This '

0

16 FE

D0239478

SANDWELL LIBRARIES

I 1373257

THE WORLD OF

Music

SANDWELL COMMUNITY LIBRARY SERVICE	
I1373257	
Cypher	21.8.00
J780	£7.99

THE WORLD OF
Music

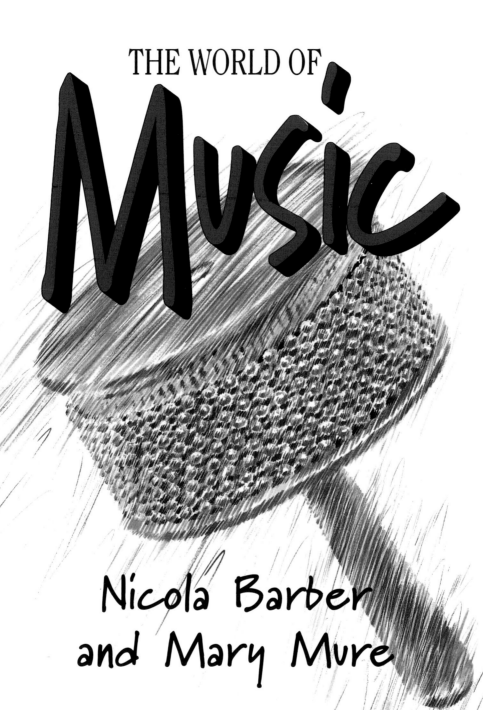

Nicola Barber
and Mary Mure

EVANS BROTHERS LIMITED

This book is dedicated to Lucy Ellen Taylor.

Evans Brothers Limited
2A Portman Mansions
Chiltern Street
London W1M 1LE

© Evans Brothers Limited 1995
First published 1995
Revised Edition 1998
First published in paperback in 2000

All rights reserved. No part of this publication may be reproduced, stored in a retrieval system or transmitted in any form or by any means, electronic, mechanical, photocopying, recording or otherwise, without prior permission of Evans Brothers Limited.

British Library Cataloguing in Publication Data.
A catalogue record for this book is available from the British Library.

Managing Editor: Su Swallow
Editor: Kate Scarborough
Designer: Neil Sayer
Production: Jenny Mulvanny
Artwork : Carl Melegari

Printed by Grafo in Spain

ISBN 0 237 52186 5

Acknowledgements

With thanks to Helen Drew for reading the manuscript.
For permission to reproduce copyright material the author and publishers gratefully acknowledge the following:
Cover (clockwise from top left) Robert Harding Picture Library, VCL/Telegraph Colour Library, Sarah Errington/The Hutchison Library, Gavin Hellier/Robert Harding Picture Library (back cover) The Bridgeman Art Library
page 8 (top) Robert Harding Picture Library, (bottom) The Bridgeman Art Library; page 9 (top) Spectrum Colour Library (bottom) Laister Dickson Ltd; page 10 (top) Giraudon, The Bridgeman Art Library, (bottom) Barry Mayes, Life File; page 11 (top) Jonathan Fisher, Performing Arts Library, (bottom) SH & DH Cavanaugh, Robert Harding Picture Library; page 12 Giraudon, The Bridgeman Art Library; page 13 (top) British Museum, The Bridgeman Art Library, (bottom) Alvis Upitis, The Image Bank; page 14 (top) Resource Foto, Redferns, (bottom) Tony Russell, Redferns; page 15 Robert Harding Picture Library; page 16 (top) Trustees of Berkeley Castle, The Bridgeman Art Library, (bottom) Robert Harding Picture Library; page 17 (top) David Hughes, Robert Harding Picture Library, (bottom) R Ian Lloyd, The Hutchison Library; page 18 Towneley Hall Art Gallery & Museum, The Bridgeman Art Library; page 19 (top) Clive Barda, Performing Arts Library, (bottom) Odile Noel, Redferns; page 20 Dulwich Picture Library, The Bridgeman Art Library; page 21 Clive Barda, Performing Arts Library; page 23 The Hutchison Library; page 24 (top) Victoria & Albert Museum, The Bridgeman Art Library, (bottom) Mary Evans Picture Library; page 25 (top) Mary Evans Picture Library, (bottom) Jeremy Hoare, Life File; page 26 Gavin Hellier, Robert Harding Picture Library; page 27 (left) James McCormick, Performing Arts Library, (right) The Hutchison Library; page 28 (top) Archiv fur Kunste und Geschichte, (bottom) Werner Forman Archive; page 29 (top) The Bridgeman Art Library (bottom) P Trummer, The Image Bank; page 30 (top) Nigel Blythe, Robert Harding Picture Library, (bottom) e.t. archive; page 31 (left) JG Fuller, The Hutchison Library, (right) ZEFA; page 32 The Bridgeman Art Library; page 33 (top) Alan Becker, The Image Bank, (bottom) David Redfern, Redferns; page 35 (top) Tim Megarry, Robert Harding Picture Library, (bottom) Odile Noel, Redferns; page 36 Juliet Highet, Life File; page 37 (top) Jeremy Hoare, Life File, (bottom) Trip; page 38 Mowy Jeliffe, Trip; page 39 (top) Juliet Highet, Trip, (bottom) Bernard Gerrard, The Hutchison Library; page 40 James McCormick, Performing Arts Library; page 41 David Redfern, Redferns; page 42 (bottom left) Michael MacIntyre, The Hutchison Library, (bottom right) Richard Powers, Life File; page 43 (top left) GM Wilkins, Robert Harding Picture Library, (top right) Peter Palmer, Trip, (bottom) Mike Maidment, Life File; page 44 Queen Productions Ltd; page 46 Bettmann, Range Pictures Ltd; page 47 James McCormick, Performing Arts Library; page 48 (top) David Hughes, Robert Harding Picture Library, (bottom) Edward Parker, The Hutchison Library; page 49 Colorific!; page 50 Mary Evans Picture Library; page 51 (top) Bibliotheque de l'Arsenal, The Bridgeman Art Library, (bottom) Harrogate Museums and Art Gallery, The Bridgeman Art Library; page 52 (top) Bettmann, Range Pictures Ltd, (bottom) Hermitage, The Bridgeman Art Library; page 54 (top) The Bridgeman Art Library, (bottom) British Library, The Bridgeman Art Library; page 55 Museo de Firenze Con'era, The Bridgeman Art Library; page 56 (top) The Bridgeman Art Library, (bottom) Pushkin Museum, The Bridgeman Art Library; page 57 (top) Church of St Agostino, The Bridgeman Art Library, (bottom) Robert Harding Picture Library; page 59 (top) Mary Evans Picture Library, (middle) Bettmann, Range Pictures Ltd, (bottom) Mary Evans Picture Library; page 61 (top and middle) Mary Evans Picture Library, (bottom) The Bridgeman Art Library; page 62 (top) Mary Evans Picture Library, (bottom) Adam Woolfitt, Robert Harding Picture Library; page 63 Historisches Museum der Stadt, The Bridgeman Art Library; page 64 (top) Giraudon, The Bridgeman Art Library, (bottom) Whitford & Hughes, The Bridgeman Art Library; page 65 Mary Evans Picture Library; page 66 Mary Evans Picture Library; page 67 (top) Caroline Field, Life File, (middle) Bettmann, Range Pictures Ltd, (bottom) Clive Barda, Performing Arts Library; page 68 (top) Popperfoto, (bottom) Clive Barda, Performing Arts Library; page 69 (top and middle) Bettmann, Range Pictures Ltd, (bottom) Juliet Highet, Trip; page 70 (top) Mary Evans Picture Library, (bottom) Helene Rogers, Trip; page 71 (top) Arthur Jumper, Life File, (bottom) Graham Harison, Telegraph Colour Library; page 72 (top) Sarah Errington, The Hutchison Library, (bottom) Mary Evans Picture Library; page 73 D Saunders, Trip; page 74 (top) Mary Evans Picture Library, (bottom) Michael St Maur Sheil, Colorific!; page 75 (top) Robert Phillips, The Image Bank, (bottom) Alvis Upitis, The Image Bank; page 78 Mary Evans Picture Library; page 80 P Ward, Telegraph Colour Library; page 81 VCL, Telegraph Colour Library; page 82 VCL, Telegraph Colour Library; page 83 Bill Varie, The Image Bank; page 87 Archiv für Kunst und Geshichte, Berlin; page 88 (top) Bettman, Range Pictures Ltd.; (bottom) Historisches Museum Der Stadt, Vienna, Bridgeman Art Library; page 89 (top) Arthur Kaufman, The Bridgeman Art Library; (bottom) Bettman, Range Pictures Ltd; page 90 (top and bottom) Bettman, Range Pictures Ltd; page 91 (top) Mary Evans Picture Library, (bottom) Archiv für Kunst und Geschichte, Berlin, Bridgeman Art Library.

Contents

Introduction   8

Instruments with strings   10
Pipes   22
Percussion   34
Electronic music   44

Medieval and Renaissance music   50
Baroque and Classical music   55
Romantic music   60
    The modern age   65

    Folk music   70

    Pulse and rhythm   76
    Pitch and melody   80

    Glossary of musical terms   84
    Glossary of composers   88

    Index   92

    Internet links   94

Introduction

This book is divided into eleven chapters. Chapters one to three tell you about musical instruments from all over the world. Some will be familiar and some you may never have heard of before. In these chapters you will find boxes about instruments of the orchestra, and some other well-known instruments that you might be learning to play, such as the piano and the guitar. Chapter four gives you information about electronic instruments old and very new. Chapters five to eight explore the history of music in the Western world from 1100 up to the present day, while chapter nine is about the music of people all over the world – working songs and music for entertainment.

This music manuscript dates from the 15th century. It is decorated with instruments, and two figures playing small, portable organs.

A 19th-century painting of Johann Strauss conducting an orchestra at a court ball.

Musicians in a gamelan orchestra in Bali. Music is an important part of life all over the world.

Finally, chapters ten and eleven introduce you to how music is put together and how it is written down.

Throughout the book there are **Key Fact** notes, which point out important information.

If there is a musical word that you find difficult in this book, you can look it up in the Glossary of musical terms at the end of the book (see pages 84-7). If you want to know about a particular composer, you can look up his or her name in the Glossary of composers (see pages 88-91).

Most of all have fun reading about music !

Key facts

Pitch: the pitch of a note is how high or low it is. Volume: the volume of a note is how loud or soft it is.

Music has changed with the development of new technology. This picture shows Peter Gabriel in concert. Members of his band play a variety of electronic instruments.

Please note!

In the instrument boxes you will see a keyboard, which shows the pitch range of the instruments in the box. Middle C is coloured in bright red.

Listen out!

This picture tells you that there is an excerpt of music on the CD that goes with this book. The caption tells you which track to listen to.

Instruments with strings

This ancient Egyptian wall painting shows a harpist entertaining two listeners. It is more than 4000 years old.

Key facts

Instruments that use strings to make sound are called chordophones.

THERE ARE MANY DIFFERENT WAYS of playing strings. Sometimes the strings are plucked with the fingers or with a hard piece of plastic or wood, called a plectrum. Sometimes the strings are played with a bow. There is also a group of instruments which have their strings hit by beaters or hammers. But whether the strings are plucked, bowed or hit, the end result is that they vibrate.

Your ears hear the vibrations of the strings as a musical note. The pitch of the note sounded by the strings is affected by the thickness of the string, its length and how tightly it is stretched. If you look at the strings on a guitar you will see that the strings with the lower pitches are slightly thicker than those with higher pitches. The strings of the double bass are far thicker and longer than those of the violin. As a result, the double bass plays some of the deepest notes in the orchestra, and the violin plays some of the highest.

Tuning strings

The strings on a musical instrument are tightened until they sound the correct pitches for that instrument. Tightening the strings in this way is called tuning an instrument. Different instruments have different numbers of strings, which all have to be tuned to the right pitch. A modern guitar has six strings, a violin has four strings. The strings on both these instruments are tuned by winding the loose end of the string around a tuning

Once a violin is strung, the four strings are tuned by turning the tuning pegs.

Key facts

The pitch of a string is determined by three things:
1. how thin or thick the string is: a thin string has a higher pitch than a thick one.
2. how tightly stretched the string is: a tight string has a higher pitch than a looser one.
3. how long the string is: a short string has a higher pitch than a long one.

Fret

The guitar has thin strips of metal, called frets, across its fingerboard, to show players where to put their fingers.

peg. The player turns the tuning peg in its hole until the string is tight enough to sound the correct pitch.

The guitar has six strings, so the guitar player can play six different notes by simply plucking the strings with one hand. But it is possible to play more than one note on each string. This is done by pressing each string down against the fingerboard with the fingers of the other hand. If you press one of the strings down, you make the vibrating part of that string shorter. You can change the length of the vibrating part of the string by pressing the string down in different places. This is called 'stopping' the string. The guitar has bars called frets on its fingerboard. These show players where to put their fingers to sound different notes. The violin does not have frets. Violinists must learn whether their fingers are in the right place by listening carefully to the pitch of the note.

Resonators

LISTEN OUT FOR a musical bow on track 1 of the CD.

The first string instruments were probably musical bows, developed from hunting bows. Musical bows were simply made from a length of string, either vegetable fibre or twisted animal hairs tied at both ends to a flexible stick. They were played by plucking or bowing the string. But early musicians soon discovered that they could increase the amount of noise produced by the bow if it was held against a hollow object, such as a coconut shell or a gourd (a dried vegetable shell). The vibrations made by the bow itself produced only a faint sound. But when the vibrations were picked up by the air inside the shell or gourd the sound became much louder. The shell or gourd was acting as a resonator. Today, musical bows are still played in Africa

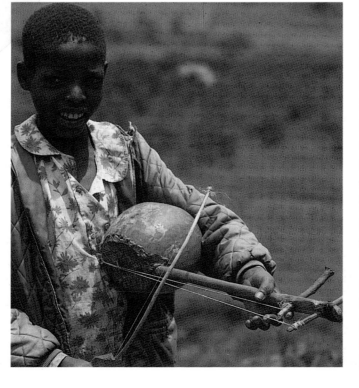

This stringed instrument has two strings attached to tuning pegs, a bow, and a resonator made from a gourd.

The hollow body of the violin acts as a resonator to make the strings sound much louder.

and Asia, and a tin can is often used as a resonator.

Modern instruments have resonators too. The strings of a violin would produce a feeble sound if they were not connected by the bridge and sound post to the front and back of the body of the violin. The hollow body of the violin acts as the resonator, picking up the vibrations of the strings and making their sound louder.

Plucking strings

One of the myths that has come down to us from the ancient Greeks tells the story of Orpheus. In one part of the myth Orpheus plays a lyre so beautifully that he persuades the God of the Underworld to allow him to take his wife, Euridyce, back from the land of the dead. Unfortunately Orpheus cannot resist stealing a look at Euridyce as he leads her back from the Underworld, although he has been forbidden to do so. As soon as he looks, Euridyce disappears once again.

The lyre that Orpheus played so beautifully is a very old instrument that was known even before ancient Greek times. Both the lyre and the harp were played as long as 4000 years ago by the people of Sumeria, the region that is present-day Iraq. We know this because both types of instruments have been found buried in the tombs of the kings of Sumeria. Pictures of musicians playing harps and lyres also appear in the wall paintings of the ancient Egyptians (see page 10).

Both the lyre and harp are played by plucking the strings. The lyre has strings attached to a resonator at one end and a crossbar at the other end. The strings are all the same length, but they are tuned by turning pegs on the crossbar. The harp has diagonal strings, attached to the resonator on one side and the neck of the harp on the

This Roman mosaic shows Orpheus playing his lyre.

A copy of a bull-headed lyre found in the ancient city of Ur in Sumeria. It would have been played around 2500 BC.

other. The strings are different lengths, and there are usually far more strings than on the lyre. Today, lyres are still played in parts of Africa, especially to accompany singing for wedding parties. Harps are played by people all over the world, and the modern harp has become an orchestral instrument.

LISTEN OUT FOR a folk harp on track 2 of the CD.

The harp

The harpist often sits behind the violins. Sometimes there are two harps in an orchestra.

The harp has the widest range of notes of all the orchestral instruments.

LISTEN OUT FOR an orchestral harp on track 3 of the CD. Other listening ideas: Tchaikovsky's 'Waltz of the Flowers' from *The Nutcracker Suite.*

THE HARP has 47 strings. Before playing the harp, the harpist must tune all the strings using the tuning pegs on the neck of the harp. The harp has seven pedals which change the pitch of the strings when they are pressed by the harpist's feet.

The harpist leans the harp against his shoulder, and puts one hand on either side of the strings.

13

The strings of the vina can be plucked with long fingernails. This musician is using a kind of plectrum attached to her fingers instead.

Indian strings

The oldest of the many string instruments played in India is called the vina (see left). The vina is mostly played in southern India. It is mentioned in one of the Vedas, holy books of the Hindu religion which date back about 3500 years. Vina players use their specially long fingernails to pluck the strings running along the fingerboard. The vina has two soundboxes, often made from gourds and beautifully decorated.

The sitar

The sitar is probably the best-known of all Indian instruments. The sitar has extra strings which give it a beautiful, shimmery sound. These are called sympathetic strings and they lie underneath the main strings. When the player plucks the main strings to play a melody, the sympathetic strings vibrate too. Even though they are not plucked, the sympathetic strings can be tuned by tightening or loosening the pegs along the side of the fingerboard of the sitar. A sitar usually has seven main strings, and between 11 and 19 sympathetic strings.

You can hear the sound of the sitar in the accompaniment to the song *Norwegian Wood* by the Beatles. The Beatles was the first pop group to try out different instruments together with the usual rock line-up of electric guitars and drum kit (see page 41).

LISTEN OUT FOR the sitar on track 4 of the CD.

Ravi Shankar is a famous sitar player. He was born in India in 1920.

14

Three Japanes kotos. You can see the movable bridges underneath the strings.

Key facts

Sympathetic strings are not played. Instead they lie underneath the main strings and vibrate when these strings are played.

LISTEN OUT FOR a zither on track 5 of the CD.

This plucked stringed instrument comes from China. It is called a p'i p'a.

Zithers from the East

An oriental zither has strings stretched along a board which acts as the resonator. The strings are plucked with the fingers or with a plectrum. Simple zithers are found all over the world, but some of the most ancient are the zithers of China and Japan. The Chinese zither is called the qin. In China, a qin was found buried in a tomb that was 2000 years old. The qin still had all 25 of its strings. Modern qins have seven strings.

The Japanese zither is called the koto. The koto was originally modelled on the qin, and it came to Japan in about AD 600. There are many traditional Japanese stories that mention the koto. In *The Tale of the Genji* Prince Genji is a skilful koto player. He falls in love with a beautiful girl who also plays the koto, but they are forced to part. He leaves her promising to be as true and constant as the middle string of his koto. (The middle string is always tuned to the same note.) Eventually they are reunited. The first sounds that Genji hears as he rides out to greet his beloved are those of her koto.

The koto has 13 strings, made from silk (or sometimes nylon). Underneath each string lies a small piece of wood, called a bridge. The koto player moves these bridges up and down the string to alter the length of the vibrating part of the string, changing the pitch.

LISTEN OUT FOR a folk lute on track 6 of the CD.

Lutes and guitars

A lute has a hollow body, which is the resonator, and a neck sticking out from the body. The strings run from the bottom of the resonator to the other end of the neck. Many different kinds of folk lute are played all over the world. In Europe, lutes became very popular in the 1600s and 1700s. The type of lute played during this period had a deep, pear-shaped back. The number of strings varied because there were many different lute designs but they were often arranged in pairs. The strings in each pair were tuned to the same pitch, so that when they were plucked together they gave a strong note. The lute was a solo instrument, and it was used to accompany songs.

The guitar was also used as an accompanying instrument. It was very popular all over Europe, but particularly in Spain. In the 19th and 20th centuries many Spanish composers have written solo music for the guitar, including Andrés Segovia, Manuel de Falla and Joaquin Rodrigo. Guitar design has continued to change as the guitar has been adapted for use in jazz, rock, folk and pop music (see page 45).

This miniature painting by Nicholas Hilliard shows Queen Elizabeth I playing the lute.

The guitar is very popular in Spain. It is often used to accompany flamenco dancing.

The guitar

The modern guitar has six strings, tuned to the notes low E, A, D, G, B and high E.

This musician is playing a classical guitar.

LISTEN OUT FOR the guitar on track 7 of the CD. Other listening ideas: Manuel de Falla's *Pour le tombeau de Claude Debussy.*

This is the range of the classical guitar.

A musician from Thailand plays a two-stringed fiddle, using a bow which is threaded through the strings.

Bowing and scraping

One of the most important musical instruments in the orchestra is the violin, a stringed instrument that is not (usually) plucked, but played with a bow. The violin is popular because it is a very expressive instrument. It can be played softly and sweetly or fast and very dramatically. The strings of the violin are sometimes plucked: this is called pizzicato. But the four strings of the violin are most usually played with a bow, made from horse hair. The violin has a long history, and many different kinds of violin are still played in various parts of the world.

Another name for the violin is the fiddle. The earliest fiddles known in Europe were small pear-shaped

The part of the violin bow that is drawn across the strings is made from strands of horse hair.

17

A fanciful painting by the 19th-century artist, Edgar Bundy, of Antonio Stradivari in his workshop at Cremona

LISTEN OUT FOR a folk fiddle on track 8 of the CD.

The pocket fiddle

The kit was a tiny violin, small enough to fit into a pocket. This was exactly what it was designed for. In the 18th century, dancing masters went from house to house to teach the latest dance. The kit provided the music for these dancing lessons. When the lesson was finished the dancing master put his kit in the pocket of his greatcoat and went to his next lesson.

instruments that were descended from an Arab fiddle called a rebab. These early fiddles were called rebecs. Instruments that look very similar to the rebec are still played in Bulgaria and Greece. Another early fiddle was the lira da braccio. This looked more like the modern violin and was held against the left shoulder. But the lira da braccio had five strings on the fingerboard and two extra strings that ran by the side of the fingerboard. These two strings are called drone strings. They were attached to tuning pegs so they could be tuned, but they could not be stopped by the player's fingers because they did not run over the fingerboard. Instead they were played as a drone – a long continuous note underneath the main melody.

The violin as we know it was first made in about 1550, and its appearance has changed very little since then. One of the greatest violin-makers was an Italian called Antonio Stradivari (1644-1737). He worked in Cremona in northern Italy, and above his house today there is a sign which says that it was he 'who brought the violin to perfection'. Some original Stradivari violins have survived, and when these are sold they fetch huge amounts of money. Stradivari also made violas and cellos.

The violin and viola

The violin has four strings, tuned to the notes G, D, A and E. In the orchestra the violins are divided into firsts and seconds. The viola is slightly bigger than the violin and has a richer tone. Because viola music does not fit very well on to the treble or the bass clef, the viola has its own clef called the alto clef. In the alto clef the middle line on the stave is Middle C.

LISTEN OUT FOR the solo violin on track 9 of the CD. Other listening ideas: Bach's Concerto for Two Violins, Brahms' Violin Concerto. You will hear the violins clearly in most orchestral pieces

The violin and the viola are tucked into the neck when played.

The violin's range and position is shown in red; the viola is shown in blue; the cello in yellow and the double bass in purple.

LISTEN OUT FOR the solo violas on track 10 of the CD. Other listening ideas: Mozart's *Sinfonia Concertante*, Berlioz's *Harold in Italy*.

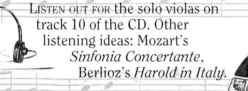

The cello and double bass

The cello has four strings tuned one octave below the strings of the viola. The cellos sit to the right of the conductor. The double bass also has four strings and stands about 1.9 metres from top to bottom. Because the double bass plays such low notes, its music is written one octave higher than the note actually sounds. The double basses sit behind the cellos in the orchestra.

LISTEN OUT FOR the solo cello on track 11 of the CD. Other listening ideas: Lloyd Webber's *Variations (on a theme of Paganini)*, Saint-Saëns' 'The Swan' from *Carnival of the Animals*.

LISTEN OUT FOR the solo double bass on track 12 of the CD. Other listening ideas: Schubert's 'Trout' Quintet. You can also hear the bass player plucking the strings in many jazz pieces.

The cello and double bass are balanced on the ground and played in front of the player.

Keyboard string instruments

If you look inside a piano you will see rows of levers, hammers and dampers. Behind them you will see the piano strings. The pianist plays the strings by pressing a key on the keyboard. The key operates a lever to move a hammer which strikes a string. So even though the pianist does not actually touch the string to sound a note, the piano, and other keyboard instruments with strings, can be classed as string instruments.

The harpsichord

The harpsichord is an older keyboard instrument than the piano. A type of 'harpsichord' was probably made as early as the 14th century, but it became well-known in the 17th century. When the harpsichord player strikes a key on the keyboard, the key moves a piece of quill (or plastic), called a plectrum. The plectrum plucks a string, making the string vibrate. The plucked strings of the harpsichord give a light, even sound. This sound was ideal for making music in the grand houses of Europe to a small audience. But when public concerts began in the late 18th century (see page 58), musicians wanted an instrument with more power.

This 17th-century painting shows a young woman playing the clavichord, an instrument similar to the harpsichord.

Hitting strings

The piano is not the only instrument that is played by hitting strings. The cimbalom is a Hungarian instrument with strings stretched over a soundbox. The strings are hit with hammers held in the player's hands. The ends of the hammers are covered in thread. The cimbalom was traditionally played by Hungarian gypsies.

The pianoforte

The name pianoforte comes from the Italian *piano e forte*, meaning 'soft and loud'. If the pianist plays the notes on the keyboard gently, the piano produces a quiet sound. If the pianist strikes the notes with more force then the sound is louder. In this way the piano was a more expressive instrument than the harpsichord, and it became a very popular solo instrument in the 19th century. The earliest pianofortes were made in the early 1700s by an Italian harpsichord-maker called Bartolomeo Cristofori.

The piano

There are many pieces written for solo piano.

LISTEN OUT FOR the solo piano on track 13 of the CD. Other listening ideas: Beethoven's 'Emperor' Concerto No. 5, Constant Lambert's *The Rio Grande*.

Only 100 years after Cristofori made the earliest pianofortes, the piano had developed to become very like the instrument that we play today. This is a concert grand piano. There are smaller sizes and upright pianos too.

The piano has a very wide pitch range.

Key facts

Instruments that use air to make sound are called aerophones.

Pipes

HAVE YOU EVER TRIED BLOWING across the top of an empty bottle? Or down a drinking straw? Try it – you should be able to make a sound. This is because when you blow into a hollow object the air inside starts to vibrate.

Wind instruments are basically hollow pipes with a mouthpiece at one end. The mouthpiece is the part used by the player to blow into the pipe. As the air vibrates inside the pipe, it produces a musical sound. In the same way that a short string produces a higher note than a long one (see pages 10-11), so the length of the pipe affects the pitch of the note. If you blow down a long pipe it will sound a low note. A short pipe will sound a high note. Compare the length of the highest wind instrument in the orchestra, the piccolo, with one of the lowest, the double bassoon. The piccolo is only 31 centimetres, but the double bassoon measures 5.6 metres! The great length of the double bassoon is folded four times in order to make the instrument easier to play.

Woodwind and brass

In the orchestra, wind instruments are divided into two sections, woodwind and brass. The woodwind section includes flutes and piccolos, oboes, clarinets, bassoons and double bassoons. The brass section includes trumpets, trombones, tubas and French horns. But the names woodwind and brass are misleading because, although some 'woodwind' instruments are made from wood, others are made from metal, and early 'brass' instruments were made from wood, horn, bark, clay and many other materials. As we shall see, the difference between the two sections lies mainly in the way that the instruments are played.

Your own wind instrument

You have your own in-built wind instrument – your voice! You can make music by simply opening your mouth and singing. You can make sound because you have two flaps of skin in your throat called your vocal cords. When air passes over your vocal cords they vibrate, producing sound.

The actual size of the piccolo compared to part of the huge double bassoon.

Key facts

The pitch of a note made by a wind instrument depends upon the length of the column of vibrating air inside the pipe.

This instrument is from Chad, Africa. The fingerholes vary the pitch as they are covered and uncovered.

Pipes and flutes

The simplest wind instrument is a pipe with a mouthpiece at one end and holes cut down the length of the instrument. These holes are covered by the player's fingers, and are called fingerholes. By opening and closing the holes the player can alter the pitch of the note. When all the holes are covered the instrument sounds its lowest note. If the bottom hole is uncovered, air escapes through the hole. This means that the length of the column of vibrating air is shorter, producing a higher note. Many different notes can be played on a single pipe by covering and uncovering the fingerholes.

Whistles and early flutes

Simple wind instruments formed from animal bones were made by some of the first human beings 20,000 years ago. These bone flutes produced whistling sounds. The native peoples of South America made clay whistles in the shapes of animals, birds and people. Another early type of flute was made up of several pipes of different lengths joined together. These pipes were called panpipes. The panpipes are played by blowing across the top of each pipe (see page 24).

As different versions of the flute appeared all over the world, many different ways of playing the instrument also developed. Some

LISTEN OUT FOR the panpipes on track 14 of the CD.

LISTEN OUT FOR a folk flute on track 15 of the CD.

Krishna plays his side-blown flute to woo a beautiful woman.

Pan tries to teach the god Apollo how to play his pipes.

were played by blowing straight down the pipe. Others, like the panpipes, by blowing across the top of the pipe. In Asia, flute players held their instruments sideways, blowing across a hole made in the side of the instrument (like the modern orchestral flute). There are many stories about the Indian Hindu god, Krishna, in which he plays the flute so beautifully that girls fall in love with him, and lost cattle make their way back to him. Perhaps the most unusual way of playing a flute is by blowing air through the nose. Nose-flutes are common in the Pacific islands of Polynesia and Micronesia.

The story of Pan

The panpipes get their name from the ancient Greek god, Pan. Pan was in love with a young girl, but she was afraid of him and tried to run away. When the other gods saw that she could not escape, they changed her into a reed to protect her. Pan was so unhappy that he made an instrument from the reed, and played upon it to console himself. This instrument became known as the panpipes.

Recorders

In Europe in the 16th and 17th centuries, a kind of end-blown flute called the recorder was very popular. The recorder was made out of wood, and had a soft, gentle sound. There were several different sizes of recorder ranging from the tiny, high-pitched sopranino to the deep great bass. Music for the recorder was often written for a group, or consort, of different-sized recorders. But in the 17th century, the side-blown flute became more popular.

Theobald Boehm invented a system of hole-coverings, or keys, for the flute.

Side-blown flutes

Side-blown flutes made at this time had open holes that were covered by the player's fingers. Gradually, flute makers added hole-coverings, called keys, to make the instrument easier to play. The most famous flute designer, Theobald Boehm (1794-1881), devised a system of keys to cover all the holes on the flute. Boehm's design has hardly been altered, and is used to make the metal flutes that are played in orchestras and windbands today.

The flute and piccolo

The woodwind section sits in the centre of the orchestra, with the flutes at the front. The piccolo is a small version of a flute that plays very high notes.

This is the flute's position in the orchestra.

This is the normal range of the flute.

LISTEN OUT FOR the orchestral flute on track 16 of the CD. You can also hear a solo flute on track 3. Listen out for the piccolo in Prokofiev's *Lieutenant Kije*.

Japanese musicians playing side-blown flutes. The flutes here are made from wood, while those used in the orchestra are usually made from metal.

A reed is a strip of cane shaped to vibrate when the player blows into the instrument.

LISTEN OUT FOR a folk clarinet on track 17 of the CD.

A snake-charmer plays a type of double clarinet to charm his snake!

Reeds in pipes

Some wind instruments have a special kind of mouthpiece which contains one or two strips of cane (sometimes plastic). These strips of cane are called reeds. When the player blows into the instrument the reed vibrates, making the air inside the instrument vibrate too. The reed makes the sound of the instrument less clear and breathy than the sound of the flute.

Some reed instruments, such as the clarinet and the saxophone, have a single piece of cane in the mouthpiece. A type of clarinet was played in ancient Egypt 3000 years ago. This was a double clarinet with two pipes joined side-by-side. Each pipe had a mouthpiece made out of a thin tube with a 'tongue' cut out that acted as the reed – vibrating in the player's mouth. Both pipes had four to six fingerholes to play tunes. Other types of double clarinet are still found in many parts of the world, including the pungi which is a favourite instrument of snake-charmers in India.

The modern clarinet

The modern clarinet was the last of the main woodwind instruments to join the orchestra. It was invented some time around 1700 by a German instrument-maker called Johann Denner. But it was not until 1800 that the clarinet joined the orchestra. It was a clarinet-maker who invented the saxophone. Adolphe Sax was trying to make improvements to the clarinet, but in doing so he designed a new instrument – the saxophone – in the early 1840s. It was soon used in military bands in France (where Sax worked).

The saxophone is a very popular instrument today. It is often played by jazz musicians.

Double reeds

Many instruments have a mouthpiece made out of two pieces of cane, shaped and tied together. This is called a double reed. The canes vibrate against each other when the player blows into the mouthpiece, making a harsh, buzzing noise. The oboe and the bassoon both have double reeds. Instruments with double reeds are much older and more widely played than those with single reeds. One instrument from Sumeria in the Middle East dates back 4800 years.

The Indian shahnai

In India, a double-reeded instrument called a shahnai is still as important today as it was 1000 years ago as an instrument to be played for dancing, and in temples and mosques. The shahnai was also played at the gates of cities to welcome important visitors. In the 14th and 15th centuries, an instrument called a shawm became popular in Europe. This double-reeded instrument

Bagpipes are played all over the world. This military bagpiper in Pakistan is performing on the Scottish Highland pipes.

Key facts

A drone is a continuous, unchanging note that is played at the same time as a melody. Many instruments have drones including the bagpipes (see below).

LISTEN OUT FOR a folk oboe on track 19 of the CD.

Bagpipes

Bagpipes are reed instruments. You might have heard Scottish Highland bagpipes, but bagpipes are also played in Asia and Africa, as well as many other European countries. Bagpipe players blow air into a bag which is held under the arm. Air is then squeezed by the player's arm out through the pipes. The pipes have reeds inside them which vibrate as the air is forced out. Bagpipe players have to blow very hard to keep the bag full of air!

had been introduced from the Middle East. Shawms made a loud, buzzing sound and were played outdoors, and to accompany dances. By the 16th century there were shawms in all sizes, including the great bass shawm which was about 2.9 metres long!

The oboe

The shawm became less popular after the introduction of the oboe, which was developed from the treble shawm. The oboe was a more refined instrument than the shawm, with a less raucous noise. It quickly became popular with composers, such as the English composer, Henry Purcell. In 1694, he wrote oboe solos into his piece *Come ye Sons of Art*. From the 18th century onwards the oboe was a regular member of the orchestra.

This early oboe has fingerholes that are covered and uncovered by the player's fingers. Modern-day oboes have keys.

Music at the Japanese court

The courtly music of Japan is called gagaku which means 'elegant' or 'correct' music. The gagaku orchestra includes wind, string and percussion instruments. The melody of the gagaku music is played by a kind of shawm called a hichikiri, and flutes. There is also an unusual wind instrument called a sho which is a mouth organ with 17 pipes that can be used to play chords. The percussion section is made up of different-sized drums and gongs, and the strings include kotos (see page 15) and a type of lute. The tradition of gagaku music has survived for over 1000 years, and it is still heard today at the imperial palace in Japan.

LISTEN OUT FOR a mouth organ like the sho on track 21 of the CD.

The clarinet and bass clarinet

The bass clarinet is twice as long as the normal clarinet, and plays lower notes.

LISTEN OUT FOR the orchestral clarinet on track 18 of the CD. Other listening ideas: the opening of Gershwin's *Rhapsody in Blue*.

This painting by the French artist, Edgar Degas, shows a bassoonist playing in an orchestra.

Playing the clarinet in an orchestra

The saxophone

The saxophone is a crossover between a brass and a woodwind instrument: it is made of metal but it has a single reed in the mouthpiece and uses keys.

Listen out for the saxophone playing as part of the orchestra on track 23 of the CD. More often, you will hear the saxophone in pop and jazz music.

The bassoon and double bassoon

The double bassoon is sometimes called the contrabassoon. It plays the deepest notes in the woodwind section.

LISTEN OUT FOR the bassoon and double bassoon on track 22 of the CD. Other listening ideas: opening bars of Stravinsky's *Rite of Spring*.

The oboe and cor anglais

The cor anglais is a larger version of the oboe with a curved mouthpiece. It plays deeper notes than the oboe.

LISTEN OUT FOR the solo oboe on track 20 of the CD. Other listening ideas: Vaughan Williams' Oboe Concerto. Listen out for the cor anglais in Dvořák's Symphony No. 9 'From the New World' playing the tune in the 2nd movement.

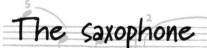

The clarinet's range and position is shown in red; the oboe's is shown in blue; the cor anglais' in yellow and the bassoon's in purple.

The organ

The organ was invented by the ancient Greeks over 2000 years ago. The first organs used water power to push air through the pipes. Today, electric fans do the same job. The biggest organs have thousands of pipes. The deepest notes on the organ are produced by pipes over 10 metres long.

Trumpet calls

In 1923, the tomb of one of the ancient Egyptian pharaohs (kings), Tutankhamun, was opened up for the first time since his death, over 3000 years ago. Inside many rich treasures were found, including two trumpets. The trumpets were about 50 centimetres long: one was made out of silver, the other out of copper. They were probably used for playing fanfares on special occasions.

The pipes of an organ in a church in Germany. The pipes vary in length and width to produce different pitches.

Roman trumpeters

Trumpets were also played by the ancient Greeks and Romans. In the Roman army, trumpets were very important signalling instruments. A long, straight trumpet called a tuba was used to accompany marching, and to sound the attack and retreat. It was also sounded in the heat of a battle in order to frighten enemy soldiers with its raucous cry! Other Roman military trumpets included the lituus which had a curled end in the shape of a 'J', and a long, looped instrument in the shape of a 'G' called a buccina. All these instruments made a loud, clear noise that could be easily heard a great distance away.

The modern trumpet has valves to produce different pitches.

Roman soldiers playing a type of military trumpet called a buccina.

Key facts

The sound of a 'woodwind' instrument is produced by blowing across or down a hole in a pipe, sometimes using a reed.

The sound of a 'brass' instrument is produced by vibrating the lips against a mouthpiece. This makes the air inside the instrument vibrate too.

LISTEN OUT FOR a folk trumpet on track 24 of the CD.

The Swiss Alphorn can be up to three metres long.

Modern trumpets

Today, long straight trumpets are still used to play ceremonial music for special occasions. But the trumpets played in bands and orchestras are folded up to make them easier to hold and play. The trumpet is a member of the brass section of the orchestra (see page 33), together with the trombone, tuba and French horn. These instruments are usually made of brass or other metals, but there is a more important similarity between them. All these instruments have a cup-shaped mouthpiece. So the main difference between brass and woodwind instruments is not the material from which they are made: it is the way in which they are played. Modern brass instruments do not have holes and keys like the woodwind instruments. Instead they have valves (see page 87).

Large trumpets

Simple trumpets are played all over the world. The native people of Australia, the Aborigines, play a type of wooden trumpet called a didgeridoo. This instrument is made out of a hollow tree branch, and it is usually about 130 centimetres long. The Swiss Alphorn can be up to three metres in length. The Alphorn is used by herdsmen in the high Alpine valleys to send signals from one valley to another.

Many brass instruments are played in brass bands including trumpets, bugles, cornets and larger instruments, such as euphoniums and sousaphones.

The trombone player pushes and pulls the slide in and out to produce different pitches.

Trombone slides

Some trombones have valves, but many trombonists play simple slide trombones. The design of these trombones has changed very little since the 1500s. A slide trombone has a U-shaped piece of tubing that moves in and out. As the player pushes the slide out, the tube becomes longer, and the trombone sounds deeper notes. As the player pulls the slide in, the tube becomes shorter and the trombone sounds higher notes. Valve trombones have a slide too, but the valves help to make the instrument easier to play. Trombones became regular members of the orchestra in the late 18th century. Early trombones were called sackbuts from the old French word *sacquebout* which means 'pull-push'.

Hunting horns

The simplest kind of horn is a curved instrument, often made out of the horn of an animal. Horns can also be made from large shells, wood, elephant tusks and metal. The sound is produced from all these different kinds of horn by the vibrations of the player's lips. Simple horns are still used in many parts of the world for sending signals, and in religious ceremonies. In Europe, horns were used for sending signals while hunting. Hunting horns were usually made from metal, coiled into a round shape. The coil fitted over the huntsman's shoulder, so that the horn could be easily carried on horseback. The orchestral French horn developed from these coiled hunting horns.

A detail from a 15th-century tapestry showing a man out hunting with his dogs. In his hand he is holding a hunting horn.

The trumpet

The brass section sits behind the woodwind in the orchestra. The trumpets often sit behind the bassoons.

LISTEN OUT FOR the solo trumpet on track 25 of the CD. Other listening ideas: Handel's 'The Trumpet Shall Sound' from *Messiah*, Gershwin's *An American in Paris*. You will also hear the trumpet played in many jazz pieces.

The French horn

The French horns sit next to the trumpets.

LISTEN OUT FOR the French horn on track 26 of the CD. Other listening ideas: Beethoven's Symphony No. 3 'Eroica' the 3rd movement, Prokofiev's *Peter and the Wolf* (three horns play the wolf).

The French horn developed from the hunting horn which curled around the hunter's shoulder. Modern French horns have valves, which help the player to sound different pitches.

The trombone and tuba

The trombones and tuba often sit at the back of the orchestra behind the trumpets.

LISTEN OUT FOR the trombone on track 27, and the tuba on track 28 of the CD. Other listening ideas: trombone trills in the last movement of Dvořák's Symphony No. 8, and the tuba in Wagner's Overture to *The Mastersingers*. You will also hear the trombone played in many jazz pieces.

The tuba is played in orchestras and brass bands, as well as in jazz bands.

The position and range of the trumpet is shown in red, the French horn's position and range is shown in blue, the trombone's is in yellow and the tuba's in purple.

33

Percussion

PERCUSSION INSTRUMENTS MAKE A SOUND when they are hit or shaken. Some percussion instruments, such as glockenspiels and xylophones, sound pitched notes when they are struck. They are called tuned percussion. Other percussion instruments simply make interesting noises without sounding any particular pitch when they are struck or shaken. They are called untuned percussion.

Simple percussion

Many percussion instruments are very simple. Stamping tubes, for example, are hollow tubes often made out of bamboo which are stamped against the ground. Different size and width sticks make sounds at different pitches. Scrapers have a notched edge which makes a rasping noise when they are rubbed against a stick. Scrapers were made by the earliest peoples out of pieces of bone, shells or even stones. In Portugal, two pine cones are rubbed together as scrapers.

LISTEN OUT FOR stamping tubes on track 29 of the CD.

Key facts

There are two groups of percussion instruments: idiophones sound when they are hit or shaken. Membranophones have a tightly stretched skin which vibrates when it is hit.

Rattles

Rattles are found all over the world and are made out of almost any material. The simplest rattles are the dried seed heads of flowers which contain rattling seeds. Some rattles have jingles attached, made out of metal discs. This type of rattle is called a sistrum. It was played in ancient Egypt, Greece and Rome, and it is still played in religious services in churches in Ethiopia, Africa.

This rattle is called a cabaca and is from South America. It has steel beads strung around the outside which move when the rattle is shaken.

34

Jingles for dancing

Jingles are often made out of a string of small metal bells, which tinkle when they are shaken. Shells, nuts and bits of animal bone are also used in different parts of the world to make jingles. Sometimes jingles are worn by dancers around the ankles or wrists. When the dancers move the jingles tinkle and provide an accompaniment to the dancing.

Clashing and crashing

Cymbals and gongs both make a loud clashing noise when they are hit hard. In the orchestra, two cymbals are often hit together to give a deafening crash at an exciting point in a piece of music. The gong, too, makes a huge noise, but it is usually hung on a stand and played with a large beater.

Morris dancers attach bells to their legs. The bells jingle as they dance.

LISTEN OUT FOR cymbals and gongs on track 30 of the CD.

Cymbals

Cymbals are mentioned many times in the Bible. One line from the Psalms says 'Praise Him upon the loud cymbals; Praise him upon the high-sounding cymbals'. The 'loud cymbals' were probably wide and flat, rather like modern cymbals. The 'high-sounding cymbals' were smaller, cup-shaped cymbals which probably made a tinkling noise.

Today, a suspended cymbal and 'hi-hat' cymbals are often part of the drum kit (see page 41) used in jazz and pop music. The suspended cymbal is called a crash cymbal because it is often hit with a loud 'crash'. It is mounted on a metal stand and played with hard sticks, or with a soft wire brush. 'Hi-hat' cymbals are also mounted on a metal stand, but they can be clashed together by operating a foot lever.

A small boy holds a pair of child-sized cymbals. Orchestral cymbals are much bigger than these.

Gongs

Gongs are very important instruments in Asia –
especially in the Far Eastern countries. Rich
families had gongs as a sign of their wealth –
owning a large gong showed that the family was
very wealthy. Some gongs were known by
names, such as 'Sir Tiger'. Gongs can be made
to different thicknesses so that they play
different pitches. In Thailand and Burma up
to 24 tuned gongs are mounted in a circular
wooden frame. This is called a gong chime.
The player sits in the middle of the frame,
and plays the gong chime with beaters.

Gamelan orchestras

In Indonesia, whole orchestras are made up of tuned
gongs, as well as other percussion instruments such as

The gong is hung up and struck with a soft beater.

A gamelan orchestra from Bali in Indonesia. The barrel drums in the foreground set the speed of the music.

Steel drums

One unusual percussion instrument comes from the island of Trinidad in the Caribbean. It is the steel drum, made from a large oil drum. The oil drum is heated and hammered so that different parts of the top of the drum sound certain notes when hit with a beater. Steel bands have up to 100 performers, each playing two or three drums. Some drums have deeper notes than others. The steel drum which sounds the highest pitches is called a ping pong. Below that is the guitar pan and the cellopan, and the deepest drum is called the boom. Steel bands play all kinds of music, from the swinging rhythms of the calypso to arrangements of music by classical composers.

A steel drum band. Different areas on top of the drum sound different notes when they are hit with a beater.

LISTEN OUT FOR a gamelan orchestra on track 31 of the CD.

LISTEN OUT FOR bells and jingles on track 32 of the CD.

Korean bronze bells. Bells that are struck with a beater are very popular in the Far East.

drums and metallophones (these are instruments like xylophones but they have metal bars). These orchestras are called gamelans. A gamelan usually has between 12 and 20 players. The instruments of the gamelan are often beautifully decorated, with metallophones in the shapes of dragons or birds, and gongs hung from stands decorated with snakes and other animals. Gamelan music is arranged according to the pitches of the instruments. All the instruments play the same theme, but the highest-pitched instruments play it at a fast speed, the middle-pitched instruments at a medium speed and the lowest instruments at a slow speed. Drum players set the speeds.

Ringing and chiming

If you have ever heard church bells, you will know that bells sound notes with different pitches. The tunes rung by church bells are called peals. In England, church bells are often rung by groups of bell ringers. Each person plays one bell by pulling on a rope to make the bell swing up or down. As the bell swings, a metal tongue inside (called the clapper) hits the side of the bell and sounds a note. The bell ringer must pull the rope at exactly the right moment to make the bell sound correctly in the peal. This is called change ringing.

The oldest bell in the world is Chinese, and it is about 5000 years old. Bells are very important in China and Japan, where they are used in temples for religious ceremonies. Temple bells do not usually have a clapper; instead they are sounded by being struck with a beater. Huge temple bells are used in Japanese temples to call people to prayer. These bells are so big that they are struck by swinging a wooden beam against the side of the bell. On New Year's Eve the sound of these temple bells marks the arrival of the New Year, as they are struck slowly from temples all over Japan.

Banging and beating

LISTEN OUT FOR a slit drum on track 33 of the CD.

Drums come in all shapes and sizes and are played in all parts of the world. Drums are made from a hollow base with a skin stretched tightly over the top. When the skin is hit by the player it vibrates, making the air inside the base vibrate too. The base acts as a resonator (see page 11). There is one kind of drum which is made from a piece of solid wood and has no skin top. This is called a slit drum. Slit drums are made from wood or bamboo which is hollowed out through a slit in the side. Slit drums are often carved

African long drums being played in Burundi. Long drums are usually made from hollowed-out tree trunks with animal skins stretched over one end.

into unusual shapes. In Japan, a slit drum in the shape of a fish is played during religious ceremonies.

Drums are used for many different purposes. Throughout history, drums have been played in battles. Sometimes drumbeats were played as signals to the soldiers to prepare to march or attack. At other times drums were used to make a loud din in order to terrify the enemy soldiers.

Japanese drums

In Japan, special types of drum provide an accompaniment for the traditional Noh theatre. Noh plays take place on a bare stage, and the

Slit drums are hollowed out of a solid piece of wood.

Drummers in Rwanda. The skins of these drums are kept taut by laces that stretch from one end of the drum to the other.

LISTEN OUT FOR a talking drum on track 34 of the CD.

The sound of juju

The talking drums are an important part of the juju groups from Nigeria in Africa. Juju mixes the sounds of the talking drums with electric guitars and percussion. The melodies and rhythms of juju are from African music, but a rock sound is added by the electric guitars.

A side drum player in an orchestra. Notice how he holds the sticks.

actors wear masks. They are accompanied by drums, a flute and a chorus. The main kind of Noh drum is called a ko-tsuzumi. It has a wooden body with a skin drum head at either end. The skins are held on by two ropes, one laced from one end to the other, and the other looped around the middle. The player holds the ropes with one hand. When the player squeezes the ropes with his hand the drum skins become even more tightly stretched. Like the strings on a guitar or violin (see page 10), when the skins are stretched more tightly the pitch of the note produced changes. The ko-tsuzumi player plays several different sounds including one that is called pon. Pon is played by squeezing the ropes hard at the exact moment that the fingers of the other hand hit the drum head. This produces a change of pitch.

Talking drums

In Africa, a similar technique is used to play the talking drums. Talking drums are played in many parts of West Africa. One kind of talking drum is called a kalengo. It has a skin stretched over both ends, and it is an hourglass shape – narrower in the middle than at the ends. The skins are held in place by laces made from pieces of leather tied tightly from one end of the drum to the other. The laces are squeezed to produce different pitches. These different pitches make the music of the kalengo sound very like some African languages. This is why the kalengo is called the talking drum. The kalengo is only one of many different kinds of drum in Africa, where the drum is an important instrument.

Orchestral drums

There are several different kinds of drums played in the orchestra. The bass drum makes a deep booming sound when it is hit. The tambourine is a type of drum with jingles attached around the edge which rattle when the instrument is hit or shaken. The timpani are tuned drums. The timpani player, called a timpanist, can change the pitch of the notes sounded by the timpani by tightening or loosening the skin of each drum. This is usually done with a foot pedal which is attached to the skin. The side drum has a completely different sound from the tuned timpani. This is because the side drum has several lengths of twisted wire (or sometimes other materials such as nylon) stretched inside the drum. This is called a snare, and the side drum is sometimes known as a snare drum. When the player hits the side drum the snare vibrates inside the drum. This gives a very clear and brilliant sound. The side drum player has to learn how to play a roll. A roll is played by tapping the drum with the drumsticks so fast and so evenly that the listener cannot hear the individual beats. To learn to play a good roll takes many hours of hard practice.

The drum kit

In rock bands and jazz groups the drummer often plays several instruments, all mounted together to form a drum kit. The drum kit is usually made up of a bass drum, a snare drum, 'tom-tom' drums, a 'hi-hat' cymbal and a crash cymbal (see page 35) as well as another suspended cymbal called a 'ride' cymbal. The bass drum lies on its side and is played by the player's foot pressing a foot pedal. The 'tom-tom' drums are small drums which give a clear, high-pitched sound. The 'ride' cymbal is tapped with a stick. Many other instruments can be added to the drum kit, depending upon the noises the drummer wants to produce. These instruments often include gongs, bongos (a kind of small drum played with the hands), and even sometimes a tabla.

LISTEN OUT FOR the tabla on track 35 of the CD.

The Indian tabla

In India, the tabla is a vital instrument in music making. The full name of the tabla is the tabla-banya, because the tabla is actually two drums – the tabla played with the right hand, and the banya played with the left. The player varies the way his hands hit the tabla to produce the sound he wants. In a group of instruments, the tabla sets the beat.

Timpani

There can be anything from two to six or more timpani in an orchestra. In Hector Berlioz's *Grande Messe de Morts* (Requiem) there are 16 timpani!

LISTEN OUT FOR the timpani on track 36 of the CD. Other listening ideas: 'Tuba Mirum' from Berlioz's *Grande Messe de Morts*, Richard Strauss's *Also Sprach Zarathustra*.

The timpani are tuned drums.

The timpanist sits at the centre back of the orchestra.

Playing tunes

Some orchestral percussion instruments can be used to play tunes. The xylophone and the glockenspiel both have bars that are hit with beaters. The bars of the xylophone are made from wood, those of the glockenspiel from metal. The bars are different lengths so that each bar sounds a different note. The bars are arranged in the same pattern as the notes on a piano keyboard. The glockenspiel has a bright, clear tone. The xylophone has a much quieter tone, so orchestral xylophones usually have hollow metal resonators (see page 11) underneath each bar, to make the sound louder.

Tubular bells

If you listen to Tchaikovsky's '1812' Overture, towards the end you will hear bell-like peals ringing out over the rest of the orchestra. This is the sound of the tubular bells. This instrument is made from a series of metal tubes hung in a

LISTEN OUT FOR the xylophone on track 32 of the CD.

A beautiful, curved xylophone from Thailand.

A large xylophone (right) being played at a festival in Guatemala, Central America.

42

frame. The tubes are different lengths to sound different pitches. The player strikes the tubes with a hammer to make a loud, clear bell-like sound.

Unusual orchestral percussion

Some composers ask for odd instruments to be included in the percussion section. Car horns, chains, a blacksmith's anvil, mugs hung from strings, and even a type-writer all make an appearance in various pieces of music. One of the most impressive 'extras' is the thunder sheet. This is a large metal sheet, often hung from a tall ladder. When it is shaken, it sounds just like thunder.

Shaping molten metal on an anvil to make a horseshoe. An anvil and a car horn (right) are just two of the unusual percussion instruments to make an appearance in the orchestra.

Orchestral percussion

Here are some examples of percussion instruments that are regularly found in the orchestra: bass drum, snare drum, cymbals, glockenspiel, xylophone, tubular bells, triangle, tambourine, gong and castanets.

The glockenspiel, played here in a brass band, is also used in orchestral works. The tambourine (left) is shaken to produce a jingling sound.

LISTEN OUT FOR the side drum on track 37, and tubular bells on track 38 of the CD. Other listening ideas: orchestral xylophone in Saint-Saëns' 'Fossils' from *Carnival of the Animals*, castanets in Bizet's *Carmen*, triangle in 2nd movement of Liszt's Piano Concerto No. 1, and cymbals in last movement of Tchaikovsky's Symphony No. 4.

The percussion section is always at the back of the orchestra.

Electronic music

MANY INSTRUMENTS PLAYED IN POP AND ROCK music today are electric instruments. The development of electronic music since the beginning of the 20th century has opened up a new world of sound. Individual instruments can produce louder sounds and a greater variety of sounds than ever before. Some composers and musicians create music in a recording studio that cannot be played 'live' in a concert. Gradually, electronic music has become part of our everyday lives.

Two types of electronic music

There are two groups of electric instruments. The first group includes the most well-known electric instrument – the electric guitar – as well as the electric saxophone, violin and flute. In these instruments the sound is still made by plucking a string or blowing down a pipe. But the sound is picked up electronically and made louder, or amplified, through a loudspeaker. The second group includes some of the earliest electric instruments to be invented, such as the telharmonium and the theremin. These instruments produce sound with electronic circuits. They make a weird, unearthly noise, completely unlike any other instrument. Included in this group are more up-to-date instruments such as the synthesizer and music generated by computers.

Key facts

Acoustic instruments are instruments in which the sound is produced by the vibrations made by, for example, plucking a string or blowing down a pipe. The sound is often amplified (made louder) by a hollow resonator. In electric instruments the sound is amplified or produced electronically.

Queen in concert. Brian May and John Deacon are both playing electric guitars.

An electric guitar

The electric guitar

The electric guitar became popular during the 1950s, and today it is one of the most important instruments in pop and rock music. Many bands have two or three electric guitars, often a lead guitar, a rhythm guitar and a bass guitar. The lead guitar plays tunes, the other two provide accompaniment. Electric guitars often look quite different from acoustic guitars. This is because an acoustic guitar must have a hollow body which acts as a natural resonator (see page 11). But the sound of an electric guitar is amplified electrically, so there is no need for a hollow body. Most electric guitars have flat, solid bodies made from wood or plastic. The body of the electric guitar must be strong enough for the strings and electrical parts to be attached to it. But it can be any shape, and electric guitars are made in many unusual shapes.

How the guitar works

If you look at an electric guitar you will see that underneath the strings is an oblong metal plate, with a small circular button positioned under each string. This is called the pick-up (some guitars have more than one pick-up). Each circular button on the pick-up is actually a magnet. Underneath the magnets is a wire coil. When the strings of the guitar vibrate, the magnets produce an electric signal in the wire coil. Wire leads take the signal from the coil to a box called an amplifier, and then to the loudspeaker. In the loudspeaker the signal is converted into the sounds that you hear. The amplifier makes the sound of the strings much louder than they would naturally be. Volume controls on the guitar and the amplifier allow the player to control exactly how loud or how soft the sounds are.

Music of the electric guitar

The electric guitar is played widely in rock and pop music, but some players have become famous for their use of the guitar, and its many different effects. Listen to the electric guitar playing of these famous performers: Eric Clapton, Jimi Hendrix, Frank Zappa, Pete Townsend (The Who), Brian May (Queen), Andy Summers (The Police), Robert Fripp and Steve Vai.

The vibraphone

Microphones

The electric violin has a pick-up, like the electric guitar, as well as a volume control. The electric flute and saxophone both have small microphones inside the instrument, attached to amplifiers. The microphone picks up the air vibrations inside the instrument and sends them as electric signals to the amplifier. The signals are increased in the amplifier before going to the loudspeaker, where they are turned once again into sound.

The vibraphone

There is one orchestral instrument that uses an electric motor to create its unusual sound. This is the vibraphone. Its top looks like a glockenspiel, with metal bars arranged like the keys of the piano. But underneath the bars lie metal tubes which act as resonators. At the top of each tube is a small propeller, like the propeller on a plane. The propeller is driven by an electric motor, and it gives the vibraphone an unusual vibrating sound. You can hear the sound of the vibraphone in Britten's opera *A Midsummer Night's Dream* and Milhaud's Concerto for Marimba and Vibraphone.

Electronic sounds

The first instrument to produce electronic sounds was the telharmonium, invented in 1906. This machine was huge – it weighed 200 tonnes and was 18 metres long. Smaller and more successful electronic instruments were developed in the 1920s and '30s. These included the theremin and the ondes martenot. The theremin was named after its inventor, Leon Theremin. It was also an unusual looking instrument, being a box with a metal rod sticking through the top and a metal loop out of one side. The electronic sound it produced was controlled by the distance of the player's hands from the rod

The Russian scientist, Leon Theremin, plays the electrical instrument that he invented, called the theremin.

and the loop. The player changed the pitch of the note by moving the right hand towards or away from the rod. The volume was controlled by how far the player's left hand was held from the loop. You can hear the strange sounds of the theremin on the recording of the song *Good Vibrations* by the Beach Boys.

The ondes martenot

The ondes martenot looks more familiar than the theremin, having a keyboard. It makes exotic, swooping sounds and is the only one of these early electronic instruments still played in orchestras today, for example in the *Turangalîla Symphony* by the French composer, Olivier Messiaen (see page 67).

Drum pad and synthesizer

Some modern electronic instruments reproduce the sounds of traditional, acoustic instruments. The drum pad, for example, is a thin plastic pad with pick-ups underneath that sense how hard the drummer hits the pad. Hitting the pad with a stick produces an electronic signal that gives a drum sound. The synthesizer, too, can reproduce the sounds of almost every instrument in the orchestra. But the synthesizer not only produces many other sounds, it also allows the musician to work with sound in completely new ways.

Playing a synthesizer. Synthesizers can store sounds and series of notes.

Working with sounds

Many synthesizers can 'sample' sounds. For example, you can sing a single note into a microphone on the synthesizer. The synthesizer will analyse, or 'sample' the sound of that single note. You can then use the sampled sound to play any note on the synthesizer. You can store your sampled sounds in the synthesizer and build up your own collection. Sequencers in a synthesizer are small computers that memorize sound. If you play a group of notes on the synthesizer the sequencer will memorize them. The sequencer will then play this musical phrase back, as many times as you want. Some sequencers can remember several musical phrases, and will play

A drum machine produces drum sounds electronically.

Sound produced by the singer in the studio is controlled by technicians working at the mixing desk (foreground).

them back in any order you want. The use of a phrase of music that is repeated over and over again is called ostinato (see page 68). Many pop musicians use sequencers to make backing tracks.

Drum machines

Some bands have done away with a drummer altogether and use a drum machine instead. A drum machine either produces a drum-like sound electronically, or uses 'sampled' drum sounds from real drums . Drum machines are used especially in disco and funk music, where a precise, unchanging beat is needed. Once a rhythm pattern has been fed into the machine, a sequencer memorizes the pattern and repeats it. Some drum machines have various common rhythm patterns already set and memorized. All the player needs to do is to set the machine to the right pattern and off it goes!

Electronic music

Many musicians have experimented with the new possibilities provided by developments in electronic instruments and computers. Some musicians have experimented with sounds recorded on tape machines, producing new and strange effects by speeding up and slowing down the sounds, recording one sound on top of another, and playing sounds in reverse. This kind of music is called *musique concrète*. The German composer, Karlheinz Stockhausen, has written a *musique concrète* piece using recordings of one boy singing and speaking. Stockhausen has altered the

MIDI

MIDI stands for Musical Instrument Digital Interface. MIDI is a computer language that allows synthesizers and sequencers made by different manufacturers to work together. With MIDI leads, you can connect up your computer, synthesizer, electric guitar and sampler and you're off!

recordings to create a new piece, with the effect of many voices singing and speaking.

Computer-programmed music

Other musicians use computer programmes to create musical sounds. One piece by Lejaren Hiller and John Cage uses seven harpsichords and 51 tapes of computer sounds. The seven performers switch on the tapes and play the harpsichord parts in any order they wish. So the overall sound of the piece is left to chance, and will sound different at every performance.

Today, electronic music is a familiar sound to us – even if we sometimes don't realise that it is electronic music! For example, the sound tracks and sound effects for films and television programmes are often created on synthesizers and computers. In Paris, an institute of electronic music (called IRCAM) opened in 1978. At the institute, musicians and composers such as Pierre Boulez and Luciano Berio work and experiment with all kinds of computer music.

Electronic rock

Many pop and rock musicians use the most up-to-date electronic equipment for recording and for their live shows. But some musicians have become particularly well known for their experiments with electronic music. You could try listening to electronic music by any of these musicians: Jean-Michel Jarre, Brian Eno, David Byrne and Peter Gabriel.

Using synthesizers and other electronic equipment, Jean-Michel Jarre performs spectacular concerts in front of huge crowds.

Medieval and Renaissance music

Music — History

1100 — 12th century

Period of troubadours and trouvères

1200 — 13th century

Period of early polyphony

Magna Carta in England (1215)

Sumer is icumen in written down about 1260

Marco Polo travels to China (1275-93)

1300 — 14th century

Hundred Years' War between France and England begins (1337)

Black Death in Europe (1347-50)

Machaut *Mass de Notre Dame* (1360)

1400 — 15th century

Dufay Mass *Se la face ay pale* (1440s)

Beginning of the period called the Renaissance
Gutenberg invents printing (1454)
Columbus sails to America (1492)

Early music printing (1476)

Josquin Desprez first book of Mass settings printed (1502)

1500 — 16th century

First Italian Madrigals

Luther attacks Roman Catholic Church (1517)

Palestrina first book of Masses (1554)

Magellan's fleet circumnavigates the world (1519-22)

Byrd member of Chapel Royal at court of Queen Elizabeth I

Reformation in Europe

Musica Transalpina published in England (1588)

Spanish Armada defeated (1588)

1600 — 17th century

Period of English madrigal

THE HISTORY OF WESTERN MUSIC is short when compared to the musical traditions of India, Africa, China and Japan. Western music has its origins in the music of the ancient Greeks and Romans. But we know little about the kinds of music that were sung and played until music began to be written down.

As in many religions, music was an important part of worship in the Christian Church. When Gregory I was pope (AD 590–604), music sung in the mass started to be collected and written down. The music was a simple kind of melody, called plainsong (or plainchant). Plainsong is still sung in churches all over the world today. It is also known as 'Gregorian chant', after Pope Gregory.

Pope Gregory I

Key facts

The mass is the central ceremony of the Roman Catholic Church. The words of some parts of the mass change, other parts always stay the same. The five sections that stay the same are called the Kyrie, Gloria, Credo, Sanctus and Agnus Dei. These are the parts that were set to music by composers such as Dufay, Josquin Desprez, Palestrina and Byrd.

Musicians provide entertainment at the house of a French nobleman.

Singers gather round a music stand to perform a piece of music.

Travelling minstrels

Churches were not the only places where music could be heard in medieval Europe. Minstrels travelled around the courts of Europe, singing songs about love and heroic deeds. In France, these minstrels were often noblemen, and they were known as troubadours or trouvères. As the minstrels sang they accompanied themselves on the harp or lyre. Many of the minstrels' songs were written down in collections, some of which still survive today.

Music in many parts

Today, we are used to hearing music which has a tune that is sung or played, and an accompaniment beneath. But the earliest plainsong had no accompaniment – it was a kind of wandering melody sung on its own. Gradually, musicians began to write music in more than one part. Sometimes one voice would sing the melody, and another voice would sing a long note or drone (see page 27) beneath. This idea developed until composers were writing music with four or five different parts, all being sung at the same time. Music with more than one part is called polyphony, from the Greek words *poly* meaning 'many' and *phone* meaning 'sound' or 'voice'.

The importance of printing

Printing was invented in the West by a German, Johannes Gutenberg, in the middle of the 15th century (the Chinese had invented printing around AD 700). Music printing began in about 1476. Before this time, music had to be copied out by hand, which took a long time and was very expensive. But printing meant that many copies of a piece of music could be made quickly and cheaply.

The madrigal

One of the most popular forms of music in the 16th century was the madrigal. A madrigal is a polyphonic piece set to poetry, with usually four or five parts sung by different voices. The first madrigal composers worked in Italy. Printed copies of their music soon spread the popularity of the madrigal across Europe. In 1588 a collection of Italian madrigals with their words translated into English was published in England. It was called *Musica Transalpina,* 'Music from across the Alps'. This collection inspired many English composers to write madrigals too.

One of the features of the madrigal was that composers used the music to illustrate what was happening in the

An early printing press of 1520. Printing enabled people to make many copies of a piece of music.

The oldest popular song

One of the oldest surviving popular songs was written down in about 1260. The song is called *Sumer* [summer] *is icumen* [coming] *in*. It was sung in a round – with one part coming in after another. It is still sung today.

Three 16th-century musicians: a lute player, a flautist and a singer.

Key facts

The term Renaissance is used to describe the period from roughly 1450 to 1600. The word Renaissance means 'rebirth'. It marks a period in European history when there was a revival in art, literature, music and learning.

words. For example, in the madrigal *As Vesta was from Latmos hill descending*, Thomas Weelkes sets the words 'came running down amain' to descending patterns of notes. A sad madrigal by John Bennet starts with the words 'Weep, O mine eyes' on long, held notes. Illustrating the words through the music in this way is called 'word-painting'.

Composing music for the Church

At the beginning of the 16th century, the Roman Catholic Church was the main religion in Europe. But in 1517, a German monk called Martin Luther nailed 95 'theses' or complaints to the doors of the church in Wittenberg in protest at corruption in the Church. He demanded reform, and he helped to start the change that is now called the Reformation.

During the Reformation many people broke away from the Catholic Church and set up their own churches. They were often called Protestants, because they protested against the Roman Catholic Church. Luther wanted the congregation to take part in church services. In the Roman Catholic Church, plainsong

In 1517, Martin Luther nailed a list of 95 complaints about the Catholic Church to the doors of the church in Wittenberg. He helped to start the change that is now known as the Reformation.

53

Queen Elizabeth I of England dances with her favourite, the Earl of Leicester, accompanied by her court musicians.

was sung by the monks and in Latin – a language that most ordinary people did not understand. Luther collected together tunes that people could easily learn, set to words in their own language. These pieces are called chorales. Sometimes Luther composed the tunes for these chorales himself.

Byrd and Palestrina

Two great composers of the Renaissance, William Byrd and Giovanni Pierluigi da Palestrina, both wrote music for the Roman Catholic Church. Byrd was a Roman Catholic in England in the reign of Queen Elizabeth I. Elizabeth was a Protestant, but she did not persecute Byrd for his religion, and even employed him as a musician in the Chapel Royal. Byrd wrote music for three settings of the Roman Catholic mass, as well as music for the Anglican (the English Protestant Church) services. Byrd's mass settings were published in England, but without a title page so that the dangerous word 'mass' did not appear. They were called 'Kyries' instead. Byrd's masses may have been performed secretly at the homes of his Catholic friends. Palestrina, on the other hand, lived all of his life in Rome, the centre of the Catholic Church. He wrote 105 settings of the mass, many dedicated to the pope.

William Byrd worked closely with another composer, Thomas Tallis, at the Chapel Royal. This is the title page to a set of pieces called Cantiones *that they published jointly in 1575.*

Baroque and Classical music

Music		History
First opera performed (1600)	1600 — 17th century	Beginning of the Baroque period
Monteverdi's opera *Orfeo* performed (1607)		Gunpowder Plot to overthrow James I of England (1605)
First public opera house opens in Venice (1637)		Pilgrim Fathers sail to North America (1620)
Monteverdi's opera *Return of Ulysses* (1641) performed in Venice		Louis XIV becomes King of France (1643)
		Charles I beheaded in England (1649)
Lully at court of Louis XIV		Isaac Newton and the theory of gravity (1687)
Stradivari making violins in Cremona	1700 — 18th century	Frederick the Great, King of Prussia crowned (flute player and musical patron) (1701)
First piano built		
Bach's 'Brandenburg' Concertos (1721)		George I of England crowned (Handel's patron) (1714)
First performance of Bach's *St Matthew Passion*		
Haydn's 'Farewell' Symphony No. 45 (1772)		Beginning of the Classical period
(1786-91) Mozart writes four great operas: *Marriage of Figaro, Don Giovanni, Cosi fan Tutti, The Magic Flute*		American Declaration of Independence (1776)
		French Revolution (1789)
	1800 — 19th century	
Beethoven's Symphony No. 3 'Eroica' (1803)		Napoleon declares himself Emperor of France (1804)

FOR THE COMPOSERS OF THE 17TH century, writing expressive music to illustrate words became very important. Composers now began to write music for a solo line with an accompaniment beneath. They also began to write music for specific instruments or voices.

The first opera

Opera began at the end of the 16th century. A group of poets and musicians in Florence, Italy, developed the idea of a dramatic work, in which all the words are sung in a very expressive way. In 1607, an opera by Claudio Monteverdi was performed in Mantua, also in Italy. This opera was called *Orfeo*, and it is still performed today. The opera tells the story of Orpheus and Eurydice (see page 12).

A view of Florence in the 16th century.

The oratorio

Just as composers were writing new, expressive music for the opera house, so they also began to write dramatic music based on religious stories. An oratorio is rather like an opera that tells a story from the Bible, with soloists representing the different characters, a chorus and orchestral accompaniment. The difference is that the singers in an oratorio do not usually wear special costumes or move around the stage. Probably the most famous of all oratorios is *Messiah* by G. F. Handel. *Messiah* tells the story of the birth and death of Jesus Christ.

Music at court

In European courts, musical entertainments were often expensive occasions. The lavishness of these musical occasions was one way of showing the world how rich and important the ruler of the court was. In the 17th century in France, King Louis XIV employed several orchestras and choirs to

George Frideric Handel sits with a score of his oratorio Messiah *on a table in front of him.*

Key facts

The word 'Baroque' is often used to describe the art and music of the period from roughly 1600 to 1750. The word 'Classical' is used to describe the music of the period from roughly 1750 to 1827 (the year of Beethoven's death).

The sumptuous court of Louis XIV at Versailles. Louis XIV employed large numbers of musicians to entertain him.

Key facts
The system of rich families paying for the services of composers and musicians is called patronage.

The crucifixion of Christ. Passion oratorios relate the events leading up to and after Christ's crucifixion.

play and sing music for different courtly occasions. These included a group of 25 violins to play during the king's dinner; another different group of 24 violins to accompany him when he went to his country houses, and to play for balls; a choir for his private chapel; and a band of wind and brass players for ceremonial music and to accompany outdoor pageants.

Bach and the Passion

One type of oratorio became particularly popular in the Baroque period. Passion oratorios told the story of the events running up to and just after Christ's crucifixion. Several composers wrote Passions, but the best examples are those written by J.S. Bach. From 1723, Bach worked in Leipzig, Germany and one of the first of his compositions to be performed there was the *St John Passion*. For this setting of the Passion story, Bach used words from St John's Gospel in the Bible, as well as some other Passion poetry.

A few years later he wrote another setting using words from the Gospel of St Matthew. Bach's Passions have a storyteller, called the Evangelist, who relates the events of the Passion. The story is broken up by choruses, solo songs called arias, and settings of chorales (see page 54). Often the chorus helps to tell the story, taking the part of the disciples at one point, and the part of the mob calling for Jesus's death at another. Bach uses the chorales and the arias to comment on the events of the story.

Church and Court

Before the 18th century, in order to earn a living musicians either had to find employment as church organists, or at court. J.S. Bach worked in the German city of Leipzig at the school attached to St Thomas's Church. He composed music for Sunday services, trained the choir and taught music in the school. Joseph Haydn, however, worked for nearly 25 years at the court of the Hungarian Prince Esterhazy. He wrote music for the court orchestra to perform, and presented himself every day to the Prince to see if he wanted music played to him.

Joseph Haydn worked at the court of Prince Esterhazy in Hungary for much of his life.

Haydn's farewell

Joseph Haydn was employed by Prince Esterhazy as his court musician in Vienna, and in the Esterhazy's summer palace outside the city. Although Haydn was treated well, he was still a servant who wore the livery (uniform) of the Prince's court. However, Haydn was a loyal and tactful servant.

When the Prince suddenly cancelled the court orchestra's summer holiday, Haydn wrote a new symphony called the 'Farewell'. It ended as each section of the orchestra in turn blew out their candles and walked out of the concert hall. Eventually only two violins remained. The Prince took the hint, and gave the musicians their holiday!

The symphony

One of the main types of orchestral music from the Classical period onwards has been the symphony. A symphony usually has three or four parts, called movements. The movements of a Classical symphony have contrasting speeds, fast and slow to give a well-ordered and balanced effect. Haydn wrote more than 100 symphonies, and Mozart about 50. Beethoven developed the symphony, even introducing a chorus and solo voices into his last symphony (number 9).

The beginning of public concerts

Up to the 17th century, composers were employed by the church or by wealthy patrons to write music. But during the 18th century public concerts began, in which ordinary people would pay to come and hear an orchestra play a symphony, or to see an opera. Concert halls and opera houses opened all across Europe, and popular interest in music increased. This change meant that composers and musicians no longer had to rely entirely on the church or the court to make their livings.

The Vienna State opera house, which holds performances for the general public, was built in the 19th century.

Mozart and his sister

Even as a young child, Wolfgang Amadeus Mozart showed his love of music. He and his sister, Marianne, both learned at a very early age how to play the harpsichord and to compose. When Wolfgang was only six years old, their father took his children on a tour of European courts. Wolfgang and Marianne played solos and duets to the courtiers. Marianne grew up to become a teacher and died in poverty in 1820. Wolfgang went on to compose some of the most famous symphonies and operas ever written. But he, too, died poor, in 1791.

The child prodigy, Wolfgang Amadeus Mozart, pictured here at the keyboard accompanying his father and sister.

Beethoven and Napoleon

In 1789 the people of France overthrew their king at the beginning of the French Revolution. These changes greatly influenced the composer Ludwig van Beethoven. The slogan of the French Revolution was 'Liberty, Equality, Brotherhood', ideas that Beethoven thoroughly agreed with. When Napoleon Bonaparte took control of the country, Beethoven thought he was a hero and called his third symphony, 'Bonaparte'. But in 1804, when Napoleon declared himself Emperor of France, Beethoven felt that Napoleon was no longer acting like a revolutionary. He angrily tore out the title page with the name 'Bonaparte' on it and called the symphony the 'Eroica' (the 'heroic symphony') instead.

Ludwig van Beethoven (above), like many other musicians, writers and artists, was greatly influenced by the events of the French Revolution in 1789 (right).

Romantic music

Music

1800 — 19th century

Beethoven's Symphony No. 6
'Pastoral' (1808)

Schubert writes earliest songs (1811)
Schubert's *Erl-king* (1815)

Berlioz's *Fantastic Symphony* (1829)

Mendelssohn's *Hebrides* Overture (1832)
Chopin's piano pieces *Etudes* and *Mazurkas* (1832)
Liszt writing and performing piano music

Arnolde Sax invents saxophone
(early 1840s)

Covent Garden opera house, London, opens
(1858)
J. Strauss 'Waltz King' in Vienna

Smetana's opera *The Bartered Bride* first
performed (1866)

Grieg's *Peer Gynt* Suite (1876)
Dvořák's *Slavonic Dances* for orchestra (1878)
Clara Schumann performs at Philharmonic
concerts in London

Metropolitan Opera opens, New York (1883)

Sibelius's *Finlandia* (1899)

Elgar's March No. 1 *Pomp and
Circumstance* (1902)

History

First steamship crosses
Atlantic (1819)

Slavery abolished in
British Empire (1833)

Electric light bulb
invented (1848)

Gold Rush in America
(1848)

American Civil War
(1861-5)

Suez Canal opens
(1869)

Telephone invented by
Bell (1876)

Phonograph (early
gramophone) invented
by Edison (1877)

Statue of Liberty
erected in New York
(1886)

1900 — 20th century

MANY COMPOSERS OF THE 19TH CENTURY became particularly concerned with expressing emotions and moods through their music.

Romantic artists and musicians were often inspired by nature, and especially by the idea of a hero struggling against wild, untamed nature. We saw that Beethoven named his third symphony the 'Eroica', and Beethoven's music marks the turning point between the orderliness of Classical music and the freedom and passion of Romantic music.

Mood music

Many Romantic composers wrote instrumental music that tried to describe a scene, set a mood or even tell a story. This kind of music became known as programme music. When Mendelssohn visited the islands off the west coast of Scotland, he was particularly impressed by the wild scenery. He

The wild and beautiful scenery in Scotland inspired Mendelssohn to write an overture called The Hebrides.

wrote an overture (a short orchestral piece) called *The Hebrides* (also known as 'Fingal's Cave') which painted a picture of the Scottish landscape through music.

Berlioz took the idea further when he wrote his *Fantastic Symphony*. He gave the symphony an extra title 'Episode in the Life of an Artist', and the story behind the symphony was based on his own life. Berlioz was madly in love with an actress at the time, and through the music Berlioz describes his passion for her. He even imagines in one movement that he has killed her and is being led to the scaffold for execution.

Felix Mendelssohn

Music for the piano

If one instrument is especially associated with the Romantic composers, it is the piano. By the 1840s the modern piano had developed – in fact there were now two types of piano, the powerful concert grand (see page 21) and the smaller upright piano. Concert grands were played in concert halls, and uprights were found in drawing rooms all over Europe where they were used for family music-making.

The virtuoso Franz Liszt was an amazing pianist. This cartoon shows what people thought he was capable of!

Composers such as Chopin and Liszt not only wrote music for the piano, but they were also talented players. Liszt, especially, delighted and amazed audiences all over Europe by his virtuosity. He wrote much piano music, including complicated reworkings of orchestral pieces to be played on the piano. One of the pieces Liszt rewrote for the piano was Berlioz's *Fantastic Symphony*.

Key facts

The term Romantic is used to describe art, music and literature of the 19th century.

Chopin plays the piano for an enthralled audience in 1829.

Women composers

'A woman must not desire to compose' – so wrote Clara Schumann in her diary in 1839. Clara Schumann was a talented virtuoso pianist who appeared in concerts all over Europe. She did compose music, mainly for the piano, but knowing that serious composition was not an accepted job for a woman, she devoted most of her energies to performing and to her family. Another talented musician, Fanny Mendelssohn, was sister to the more famous composer, Felix. Both children were trained in music, and Fanny advised her brother throughout his career about his musical compositions. She wrote some music of her own, but there was little opportunity for her to perform it. Although she was a talented pianist, her family only allowed her to play once in public, when she performed one of Felix's piano pieces.

Clara Schumann was a talented concert pianist, and a composer.

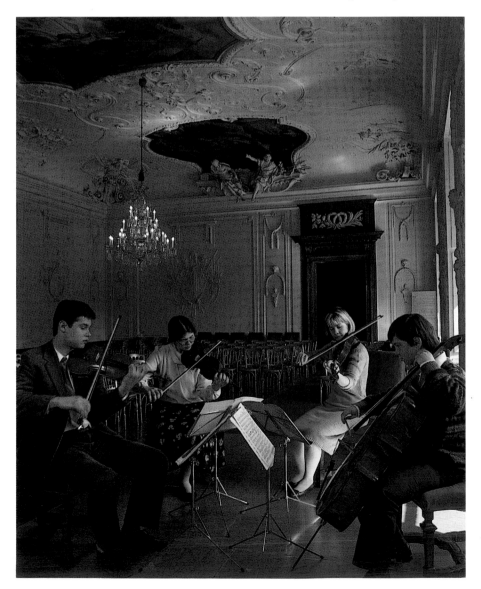

During the Romantic era a lot of music was written for smaller groups of musicians, such as the quartet. The quartet is made up of two violinists, a viola player and a cellist.

Chamber music

Music written for small groups of instruments is often known as chamber music. The most usual chamber music groups in the Classical period were string quartets (two violins, one viola and a cello), and string trios (violin, viola and cello). Haydn wrote about 70 string quartets and Mozart 26. In the Romantic period composers continued to write for string quartets, as well as music for other combinations of instruments. For example, Schubert's 'Trout' Quintet is for violin, viola, cello, double bass and piano, and his Octet (eight instruments) is for clarinet, French horn, bassoon, two violins, viola, cello and double bass.

Schubert's songs

In his short life (he died when he was only 31), Schubert wrote over 600 songs, as well as operas, symphonies and chamber music. Many of the songs are about love; others tell dramatic stories. One of the most exciting of Schubert's songs is called *The Erl-king*. It tells the story of a father carrying his young son on horseback through a wood. They are riding frantically 'through night and storm' in order to escape from the wicked erl-king (king of the goblins). Eventually the erl-king appears in front of the child and kills him. The noise of the horse's hooves is heard in the pounding notes on the piano, which stop suddenly and dramatically as the boy dies at the end. Other Romantic song writers included Robert Schumann, Johannes Brahms and, later in the century, Hugo Wolf.

An evening of Schubert's music at the house of Joseph Spaun in 1868.

Dancing music

In coffee-houses, ballrooms and salons in 19th-century Europe everyone wanted to dance the waltz. It originally came from a German and Austrian folk dance called a ländler. But it was taken up by fashionable society in the 19th century, and became very popular. Many composers wrote music for people to waltz to, but the most famous waltz-composer was Johann Strauss, who was called 'The Waltz King' in his home city, Vienna.

Dancing the waltz at a court ball in 19th-century Vienna.

63

Nationalism in music

During the 19th century, people in many European countries became more aware of their national identity and traditions. Many composers reflected this new interest in nationalism by looking back to the folk music of their country. In Russia, composers such as Nikolai Rimsky-Korsakov made use of Russian folk tunes in their music, and based their operas on Russian history. In Czechoslovakia, Bedrich Smetena, Antonín Dvořák and Leoš Janáček all chose nationalist subjects for their operas and programme music (see page 60). Other nationalist composers included Edvard Grieg in Norway, Jean Sibelius in Finland, and in England – Edward Elgar.

The Norwegian composer, Edvard Grieg.

The orchestra

The size of the orchestra grew rapidly during the 19th century. At the end of the 18th century, Haydn and Mozart were writing symphonies for orchestras of about ten different instruments, with a total of about 47 players. At the end of the 19th century, the score of *Don Juan* by Richard Strauss calls for 21 different instruments, with a total of around 99 players.

The orchestra of the 18th century was usually directed by the lead violinist. As the orchestra grew and the music became more complicated, it became too difficult to play and control the orchestra. So the role of the conductor developed.

The conductor of an orchestra was, at one time, also the leading violinist.

The modern age

Music

Puccini's opera *La Boheme* (1896)

Elgar's oratorio *Dream of Gerontius* (1900)

Scott Joplin's *The Entertainer* and *Elite Syncopations* (1902)
Debussy's *La mer* (1905)

Mahler's 8th Symphony first performance (1910)
Richard Strauss's opera *Der Rosenkavalier* (1911)
Stravinsky's *Rite of Spring* (1913)

Louis Armstrong makes jazz recordings with *Hot Five*
Gershwin's *Rhapsody in Blue* (1924)
Copland's Piano Concerto (1926)

Prokofiev's *Peter and the Wolf* (1936)

Messiaen's *Turangalîla* Symphony (1948)

First electronic music studio built (1951)
Messiaen's *Réveil des Oiseaux (*The waking of the birds*)* piano and orchestra (1953)
Stockhausen's *Gesang der Junglinge (Song of the Young Boy)* (1957)
Bernstein's *West Side Story* (1957)
Early synthesizers built

Beatles' first single *Love Me Do* (1962)
Motown music
Berio's *Sequenza III* (1966)

Reich's *Drumming* (1970-71)
Heavy metal/Glam rock/Disco
IRCAM opens in Paris (1978)
Punk/ Rap
CDs invented

Glass's opera *Akhnaten* (1984)
'Live Aid' concert

House/Rave music

History

Paris Exhibition and Eiffel Tower built (1889)

1900 — 20th century

Model 'T' Ford car produced (1908)

Amundsen reaches South Pole (1911)
Titanic sinks (1912)
Panama Canal opens (1914)
World War I (1914-18)

First films with sound (1927)

Hitler becomes Chancellor of Germany (1933)
First regular BBC TV service begins (1936)
World War II (1939-45)

Sputnik, first satellite launched by Russians (1957)

First man in space – Gagarin (1961)
President Kennedy shot (1963)
Martin Luther King killed (1968)
Americans put first men on the moon (1969)

First supersonic flight by Concorde across the Atlantic (1976)

Wreck of *Titanic* found (1985)
Berlin Wall comes down (1989)

Nelson Mandela released from prison (1990)

War in Yugoslavia (1992)

The scene at the end of Puccini's opera Madame Butterfly. *Madame Butterfly lies dead while Pinkerton comes to claim his child.*

AT THE END OF THE 19TH CENTURY and the beginning of the 20th, many composers continued to write music in the Romantic style. Works by these late Romantics include the symphonies of Gustav Mahler, the operas of Giacomo Puccini and Richard Strauss, and the oratorios and symphonies of Edward Elgar. But at the same time, new styles and new ideas were being tried out by other composers. These new ideas opened up the possibilities of the modern age.

Debussy and the gamelan orchestra

The French composer, Claude Debussy.

In 1889, Claude Debussy visited the Paris Exposition. This was the huge exhibition for which Gustave Eiffel built his famous tower. At this exhibition, there was an Indonesian gamelan orchestra (see pages 36-37) and Debussy was fascinated by the sound of the gongs, the complex rhythms and the strange scales that he heard. Debussy experimented in his own music with these new sounds and rhythms, producing music that was quite different from that of the Romantic composers. In his orchestral piece *La Mer* ('The Sea'), written in 1905, Debussy used subtle rhythms and unusual scales.

Uproar at the ballet

In 1913, some people in the fashionable audience at a Paris theatre were so upset by what they heard from the orchestra and saw on stage that some walked out and others started to shout and fight. The piece that caused this uproar was a ballet, *The Rite of Spring* by Igor Stravinsky. The subject of the ballet shocked the audience – a ritual celebrating the coming of spring in which a young girl dances herself to death. The music also shocked them, most of all because Stravinsky used irregular rhythms, often changing the time signature (see page 86) almost every bar. This use of rhythm was an important influence on many 20th-century composers.

The Eiffel Tower was built for the 1889 Paris Exposition.

The age of jazz

In the south of the USA, another new type of music was developing at the beginning of the 20th century, called jazz. Jazz grew out of the many kinds of music that were played by people in the city of New Orleans, Louisiana. Two of the most important influences on early jazz were the blues and ragtime. The blues was a kind of folk music, sung by the descendants of the people brought from Africa to work on plantations in southern USA. The words of blues songs were often about sadness and loneliness. Ragtime was a kind of piano music. Unlike the blues, it was often written down. Scott Joplin was a famous ragtime composer who wrote *The Entertainer* and *Elite Syncopations*.

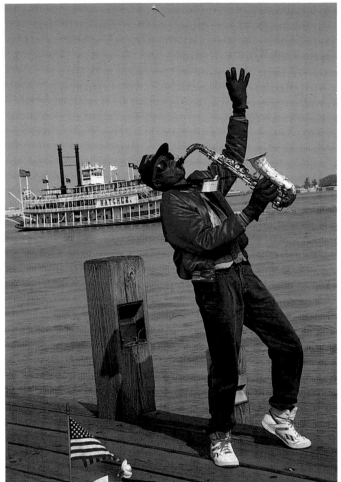

A saxophonist in New Orleans, the birthplace of jazz music.

Jazz music is often based on a tune called the theme. The performers play through the theme together to start, and then each player takes it in turns to make up a solo based on the theme. The piece often ends up with all the performers playing the theme together again.

The jazz composer and pianist, Scott Joplin.

Olivier Messiaen collected birdsong from all parts of his native France.

Messiaen's bird music

Olivier Messiaen was a French composer who is known especially for his organ music and his huge orchestral work, the *Turangalîla* Symphony which features the strange electric instrument called the ondes martenot (see page 47). One of Messiaen's first loves was birdsong. He travelled all around France to listen to birdsong. He collected the songs not with a tape recorder but by writing them down, and he used birdsong music in many of his pieces.

Key facts

Music that experiments with ostinato effects is often known as minimalist music.

The American composer, Steve Reich

Ostinato music

When a group of notes or a certain rhythm is repeated over and over again it is called an ostinato (see page 85). Many musicians have experimented with ostinato effects, including the composers Steve Reich, John Adams and Philip Glass. Reich, like many composers before him, is influenced by the subtle rhythms of the Indonesian gamelan orchestra as well as by African drumming. His piece *Drumming* uses ostinato effects on drums, glockenspiels and marimba (a large xylophone). Philip Glass has studied Indian music and he uses slowly changing ostinato patterns in his music too. He has written an opera called *Akhnaten* about ancient Egypt.

Rock and pop music

One of the major developments in the music of the 20th century has been that of rock and pop music. Of course there has always been 'popular' music, but the invention of recording and broadcasting has meant that people all over the world can now listen to the same music. There are many

A performance of Philip Glass's opera Akhnaten

different styles of pop music. You can find out about reggae on page 73, African juju on page 40, folk-rock on page 75 and Country and Western music on page 75.

Heavy metal dates from the late 1960s. Heavy metal bands play at an extremely loud volume, often using a piercing electronic sound called feedback caused by playing electric guitar in front of a loudspeaker. Heavy metal bands include AC/DC, Iron Maiden and Black Sabbath.

Motown music originated in the American city of Detroit, which has a large car manufacturing industry (motor-town). Record companies in Detroit promoted the Motown sound which was tuneful and catchy. Motown was very popular in the 1960s. Motown artists include Diana Ross and the Supremes and Stevie Wonder.

Rap became popular during the 1980s. Rap music uses a drum machine drumbeat, 'scratching' which is done by dragging the needle of a record player across a record, and rhythmic talking over the top. Artists included the Beastie Boys and Grandmaster Flash.

Spectacular costumes and stage acts are often just as important in **glam rock** as the music. Famous glam rockers included David Bowie, Sweet, Spandau Ballet and Bon Jovi.

Diana Ross and the Supremes were highly successful Motown artists.

Osibisa is famous worldwide.

Glam rock in 1973. David Bowie on stage.

Disco music is dance music, with a heavy beat. Disco music was popular in the 1970s but other forms of dance music have since taken over, such as acid house, and rave music. Disco greats included the Bee Gees, who provided the soundtrack for the film *Saturday Night Fever*.

Punk was partly a reaction to the sophisticated sounds of the disco music of the '70s. It was meant to shock. Famous punk artists included The Sex Pistols.

Many musicians in the West have become interested in the music of other cultures. Some musicians have mixed in elements from these cultures with their own music. And some African and Arab musicians have had successful record releases in the West, including Youssou N'Dour, Ofra Haza and Osibisa. This kind of music is known as **World music**.

Folk music

Some tunes that are well-known today are very old. Many Christmas carols, for example, are based on tunes and words that have been sung for hundreds of years. Often, no one knows who wrote these tunes or where they came from. They have been sung and played by generation after generation, changing slightly as they have been passed down through history. This is folk music.

Every year, carol singers sing traditional Christmas carols.

Key facts

Music of the church and the court is often known as 'art' music. Music sung by the ordinary people, that is not usually written down but passed on and changed from one generation to the next is often known as 'folk' music.

Working songs

People from different countries and cultures have their own traditions of folk music. But, although a folk song from Japan and one from South America might sound very different, the subjects that people sing about are often similar. In folk music traditions all over the world there are working songs, songs about love, everyday life, the seasons, battles and war, shepherd's songs, cradle songs and many more.

Shanties

Some of the most well-known working songs were sung at sea by sailors working on sailing ships. These songs are called shanties. Shanties were sung by sailors as they hauled on the ropes that hoisted the sails. The rhythm of the songs helped the sailors to pull together, and to raise the sail more easily. There were also shanties for other jobs on board ship, such as

All over the world, fishermen have their own songs to help them pull in their nets.

Gospel music developed from the spirituals sung by black American slaves.

pulling up the anchor. In North America, the fur traders who lived in the far north sang songs as they paddled their canoes across the icy seas. Often the song would last as long as the journey lasted, sometimes from morning to night!

Working the land

On land, many working songs helped people to forget their aches and pains as they toiled in the fields. Often these songs were about the crops being tended, or the animals being looked after. Shepherds sang about their sheep and lambs, and about the bitter weather they must endure out in the fields. In Japan, there are many songs about rice-growing because rice was one of the main ingredients of the Japanese diet. Rice-planting songs have words about putting in the rice seedlings, and how much rice they will produce. Many of these folk songs are still sung today in Japan, especially at festivals and celebrations.

Spirituals

Spirituals were religious songs sung by the black slaves working in the plantations in the southern states of the USA in the 19th century. Spirituals were sung in church, or in the fields as the slaves worked. A leader would sing one line to which the rest of the singers responded, another line and another response, and so on. The words of the spiritual songs often reflected the hard life of the slaves. Spirituals such as *Sometimes I feel like a motherless child* and *Nobody knows the trouble I seen* were sometimes called 'sorrow songs'. The same 'call and response' is used today by evangelist worshippers and is known as gospel music.

A rice-planting festival in Osaka, Japan. Traditional rice-planting songs are still sung in some parts of Japan.

71

Chinese opera

Like opera in the West (see page 55), Chinese opera is a mixture of music and drama. The opera performed at the emperor's court was very formal, sometimes lasting five or six hours. A rather different form of opera was popular with the ordinary Chinese people. Chinese folk opera often included acrobatics and mime, as well as dancing and singing. Performers were trained to sing and dance, and to perform acrobatics.

A character from a Chinese folk opera.

Music for entertainment

Once the day's work was over, it was time for some entertainment. In Scotland, before the 18th century, rich families in the Highlands paid for a storyteller, called a bard, to live as one of the household. The job of the bard was to sing and tell stories in the evenings for the entertainment of the family and their guests. Sometimes the bards were accompanied by the clarsach, a small harp, played by skilled harpists who travelled from place to place visiting the wealthy Scottish families. For dancing, a fiddler would play to accompany the whirling dances known as reels. Reels are still danced today.

Whirling Scottish dances are known as reels.

Reggae

Reggae comes from the island of Jamaica in the Caribbean. The rhythms and instruments of reggae show influences not only from Jamaican music, but from Africa and America too. The most famous of all reggae musicians was Bob Marley, who made this style of music internationally known in the 1970s.

The late Bob Marley is the most famous of all reggae musicians.

Dancing

Folk tunes were often used as music for dancing. People danced for entertainment, for celebrations, during religious ceremonies and on many other occasions and they still do! You may have seen local folk dances such as Morris dancing (see page 35) or maypole dances.

Every country has its own traditions of folk music and dancing, and when people from one country move to a new part of the world they take their traditions with them. The music and dances of the Caribbean region show the influence of the local peoples, and all the various people who settled there. In the 16th century people from many European countries colonized the islands, and from the 16th to the 19th centuries enslaved Africans were forced to work on plantations in the region. The music and the instruments of the Caribbean reflect all these different influences. For example, on one of the Caribbean islands, the Dominican Republic, Congo groups play music that mixes African drumming styles with Spanish-type melodies.

Collecting folk music

In many places, traditional folk songs and dances have been dying out since machines began to take over the work once done by hand. But at the beginning of the 20th century, some composers and musicians became interested in folk traditions, and tried to record folk tunes before they died out. The composers Béla Bartók and Zoltán Kodály travelled around Hungary recording folk music. Bartók took with him a simple recorder into which people sang or played. Bartók would then

Béla Bartók travelled around Hungary with his fellow composer, Zoltán Kodály, collecting folk music.

listen to the recording and write down the notes that he heard. Between them, Kodály and Bartók collected about 15,000 tunes, and the influence of Hungarian folk music can be heard in their own music. Another composer, Leoš Janáček, collected the folk music of his native Czechoslovakia, and in Britain Ralph Vaughan Williams, Gustav Holst and Cecil Sharp all made folk music collections.

The development of folk festivals and music

There are many festivals of folk music, but one of the most famous is the eisteddfod held every year in Llangollen, Wales. In medieval times, gatherings of bards met to discuss music and literature. The eisteddfod developed from these meetings. At the International Eisteddfod, folk choirs and dancers from all over the world compete for prizes.

There is also a National Eisteddfod held annually in different places in Wales which gives prestigious prizes for choral singing and other music.

Although many traditional folk tunes have been forgotten, folk music is still sung and played all over the world. One of the main features of folk music is that it is changing all the time. Even when folk music is written down, folk musicians invent new words, add decorations to the tune, or perform the music slightly differently each time. In many parts of the world the rhythms and tunes of traditional music have been adapted for more up-to-date instruments.

Bards at the Welsh National Eisteddfod in Aberystwyth, Wales.

Country and Western music

Country and Western music has its roots in the folk music of North America, although it is popular all over the world. Early styles of Country and Western music used the tunes of folk songs and dances accompanied by banjos, guitars, violins and mouth organ. In the 1950s a new instrument – the Hawaiian guitar – was added. This was a type of electric guitar which made an unusual sliding sound when the player dragged a piece of metal along the strings. Today, Country and Western bands still use the Hawaiian guitar as well as other electric instruments. You will probably know the names of some Country and Western stars, such as Garth Brookes, Dolly Parton and Linda Ronstadt.

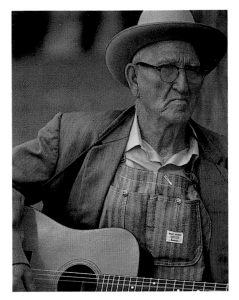

A Country and Western musician plays the guitar to accompany himself when singing.

Folk groups

Many singers and groups still perform traditional folk music, often now with the accompaniment of electric instruments. In the 1960s, a type of music called folk-rock became popular. Folk-rock music combined the melodies of folk music with the sound of the electric bass guitar and the drum kit. Often, the words of folk-rock songs carried a political message. Bob Dylan is probably the most famous folk-rock musician. Here are some other singers and groups for you to listen to: Simon and Garfunkel, Fairport Convention, Steeleye Span, Ralph McTell, Richard Thompson, June Tabor, The Chieftains, Pete Seeger and The Weavers.

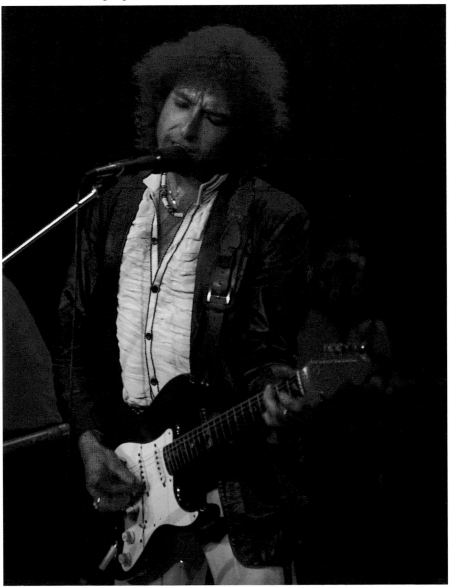

Many of Bob Dylan's songs have a political message.

Pulse and rhythm

Finding the pulse

A pulse is a steady beat. You can find your own pulse on the inside of your wrist, or on your neck underneath your jawbone. This regular beat is caused by your heart pumping blood around your body. Many everyday things also have a pulse, for example the regular ticking of a clock or the beeping of an alarm clock.

The steady beats of music are grouped together, most commonly into twos, threes and fours. When music is written down the groups are divided into bars which are separated by barlines, with the first beat in each bar being the strongest.

1 2 3 4 | 1 2 3 4

1 2 3 | 1 2 3 | 1 2 3

1 2 | 1 2 | 1 2 | 1 2

Clapping the beat

You could try inventing a 'pulse piece' with a couple of friends. It works like this: person one claps the steady pulse grouped in threes or fours. For example, use a pulse grouped in fours. Person two claps on beats 1 and 4. Person three claps on beats 1 and 3. Try the same method with different pulse groups. This gives you an idea of how music starts to be formed.

Person 1. ♩♩♩♩ | ♩♩♩♩ | ♩♩♩♩

Person 2. ♩ 2 3 ♩ | ♩ 2 3 ♩ | ♩ 2 3 ♩

Person 3. ♩ 2 ♩ 4 | ♩ 2 ♩ 4 | ♩ 2 ♩ 4

Working out the beat

Listen to different pieces of music to see if you can work out how the beats are grouped. Here are some examples of songs you may know and what pulse they have:

$\frac{2}{4}$ What shall we / **do** with the / **drunken** / **sailor**

$\frac{3}{4}$ **Close** every / **door** to me
(from *Joseph and his Amazing Technicolour Dreamcoat* by Andrew Lloyd Webber)

$\frac{4}{4}$ We all live in a / yellow submarine (by the Beatles)

Skipping the beat

Sometimes composers want to disturb the regular beat of a bar to make the music more exciting. This is done by upsetting the regular pulse of a piece of music and moving the accents from the important beats of the bar. This is called syncopation. It is used quite a lot in jazz. Scott Joplin (see page 67) wrote many pieces for the piano with jagged, syncopated rhythms. A dance, called *Elite Syncopations*, has been set to this music, which works brilliantly with the strong off-beats.

A metronome is used by musicians to help them keep to a steady pulse. It can be set to different speeds.

Music for dancing often has a very strong pulse.

Rhythm

As you sing, play or listen to music, you will notice that there is more to it than just a steady beat. There are notes that are shorter and longer than one beat. When all the notes of varying length are put together the music has a rhythm. Sometimes the rhythm of the music has a strong, steady beat or pulse. At other times there will only be a weak pulse, or there may even be no pulse at all.

The rhythm of a piece is written down in notes. These are some of the most common notes:

semibreve	𝅝	(whole note)
minim	𝅗𝅥	(half ½ note)
crotchet	♩	(quarter ¼ note)
quaver	♪	(eighth ⅛ note)
semiquaver	𝅘𝅥𝅯	(sixteenth ¹/₁₆ note)

As you will see, there are two names for each note. The names on the right show how long the notes are compared to each other. The whole note lasts twice as long as the half note; a half note lasts twice as long as a quarter note and so on.

Key facts

Quavers and semiquavers are joined together into groups if there is more than one of them. For example, two quavers are equal to one crotchet beat:

♫ = ♩

and four semiquavers are equal to one crotchet beat:

𝅘𝅥𝅯𝅘𝅥𝅯 = ♩

You can mix up different kinds of note in one beat group. For example, one quaver and two semiquavers are equal to one crotchet beat:

♪𝅘𝅥𝅯 = ♩

The time signature

At the beginning of a piece of music there are two numbers, one above the other. This is called the time signature and it explains two things. The top number tells you how many beats there are in each bar of the piece. The bottom number tells you which note is considered to be the beat in the piece. So, if a time signature says $\frac{2}{4}$, there are two beats in each bar and the beats are crotchet beats (the 4 referring to a ¼ note). If the time signature says $\frac{3}{2}$, there are three beats in each bar and the beats are minims (the 2 referring to a ½ note). You can see some examples of rhythms in these times in the box opposite.

Taking a rest

In music the silences are just as important as the notes, especially if you are singing or playing a wind or brass instrument – you need to take a breath every now and then! The silences, or rests, can have different lengths just like notes. They are written down like this:

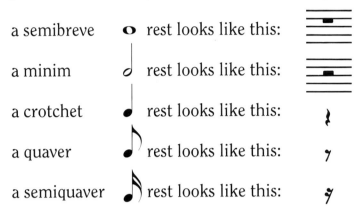

a semibreve   𝅝   rest looks like this:

a minim   𝅗𝅥   rest looks like this:

a crotchet   ♩   rest looks like this: 𝄽

a quaver   ♪   rest looks like this: 𝄾

a semiquaver   𝅘𝅥𝅯   rest looks like this: 𝄿

Going dotty

𝅝. = $1\frac{1}{2}$ semibreves
𝅗𝅥. = $1\frac{1}{2}$ minims
♩. = $1\frac{1}{2}$ crotchets
♪. = $1\frac{1}{2}$ quavers
𝅘𝅥𝅯. = $1\frac{1}{2}$ semiquavers

Sometimes you might want a note to last for longer than one beat but less than two beats. To make a note last $1\frac{1}{2}$ beats, it should be written down with a dot next to it like this: ♩. The note is a crotchet, and the dot adds on half the value of the note it is beside. You can put a dot next to any kind of note, and it will always make the note worth half as much again.

Rhythmic clapping

With a friend, try clapping these rhythms.
The first person claps:

Now try these rhythms.

The second person claps:

In bar 2 the minim lasts for the same amount of time as two crotchets. So the first person will clap twice, while the second person will clap once and wait.

In bar 4, the semibreve lasts for the same amount of time as two minims. So the first person will clap twice and the second person once and wait.
  Make up your own rhythms and perhaps try them out on percussion instruments.

Pitch and Melody

The choir of King's College, Cambridge, singing tunefully and rhythmically!

PULSE AND RHYTHM ARE NOT THE ONLY THINGS that make up a piece of music. Most popular pieces also have a good tune.

Melodies tend to go up and down in a mixture of steps and leaps, and it is the balance of steps and leaps that makes for a memorable tune. Imagine a staircase of steps, numbered one, two, three, four and so on from the bottom upwards. You could describe a melody by the number of the step, but although the numbers would tell you how the notes are arranged into a melody they would not tell you about the rhythm of the music. If you want to be absolutely clear about the pitches and the rhythm of your tune, then you have to use a more precise system of writing music down. Today, music is usually written down using five lines, called a stave.

A stave is used to write musical notes on. Each line and each space between the lines represent different pitches.

Shapes in melodies

When the notes of a tune are written on to the stave, they do not only show you the pitch and the rhythm of the melody, but also its shape. Some bits of a melody may be repeated; other bits may be different to provide contrast.

Many songs fall into a pattern of repeating one idea (A), slotting in a new idea for contrast (B), and then repeating the first idea again (A). This gives many melodies the shape AABA. It makes inventing melodies much easier when you realise that you really only need two musical ideas!

The treble clef

At the beginning of every piece of written music there is a clef. This acts as a reference point for music, because without a clef you cannot say what the pitch of any written note is. The treble clef, or G clef, shows that the second line up in the stave is a G. The centre of the clef curls around the second line up. In the middle of the piano keyboard is the note Middle C. The treble clef also tells you that any note you put on to the second line up will sound as the pitch of the first G you come to above Middle C.

In music, the first seven letters of the alphabet are used to describe notes. As you move up the stave, you go higher in pitch and forwards through the alphabet using all the lines and spaces on the stave. When all seven letters are used up, start again at A. If you want to write Middle C on the stave, you have to add an extra line. This is called a ledger line.

Middle C

C D E F G A B C D E F G

A flautist reads music that is set in the treble clef, because the flute's pitch range is higher than Middle C.

81

A double bass player reads music written in the bass clef because the double bass produces notes below Middle C.

The bass clef

To show that the pitch of the notes on the stave are below Middle C, the bass clef, or F clef, is used. The bass clef shows that the second line down on the stave is an F, the F below Middle C. The two dots sit either side of the F line.

If you look at some music written for the piano, you will usually see two staves, joined together, the top stave with a treble clef and the bottom stave with a bass clef. The stave with the treble clef is played with the right hand and the stave with the bass clef is played with the left hand.

Other instruments use the clef that is most suited to their pitch range. A flautist reads music in a treble clef, because the notes the flute can play are all above Middle C. A double bass player reads music in the bass clef, because most of the notes the double bass can play are lower than Middle C.

C B A G F E D C B A G F

Tones and semitones

On the piano keyboard, when you move stepwise from one note to the very next note this distance is called a semitone. The distance between B and C is a semitone; the distance between D and the black note immediately above it is also a semitone. The distance of two semitones is called a tone, for example F to G, or C to D.

A pianist playing the piano. The right hand usually plays above Middle C in the treble clef and the left hand usually plays below Middle C in the bass clef.

When you see this sign # in front of a note it means that you raise the note by a semitone. So if you see F#, you would play this black note on the piano keyboard:

When you see this sign ♭ in front of a note, it means that you flatten the note by a semitone. So if you see B♭, you play this black note on the piano keyboard:

Scales

A scale is a series of notes arranged in order of rising or descending pitches. There are many different kinds of scales, for example a pentatonic scale is made up of five notes, such as C, D, E, G, A or G, A, C, D, E. A raga is another kind of scale used in Indian music. Most Western music is based on major or minor scales. A major scale is a succession of notes rising stepwise with the following pattern of intervals: tone, tone, semitone, tone, tone, tone, semitone.

A minor scale is a succession of notes rising stepwise with this pattern of intervals: tone, semitone, tone, tone, semitone, tone, tone. It does not matter what note you start on so long as you follow the pattern.

A piece of music that is based on the scale of C major is said to be in the key of C major. A piece of music that is based on the scale of G minor is said to be in the key of G minor.

Glossary of composers

Adams, John (b. 1947) American composer and conductor. His works include the opera *Nixon in China*.

Bach, Johann Sebastian (1685-1750) German. One of the greatest composers, who came from a family of musicians. For much of his life, Bach worked at St Thomas's Church and school in Leipzig where he composed music for church services, as well as works such as *St John Passion*, *St Matthew Passion* and the Mass in B minor.

Barber, Samuel (1910-81) American. One of America's most popular composers who wrote extensively for the voice, as well as for instrumental groups. His most famous work is probably the Adagio for Strings.

Bartók, Béla (1881-1945) Hungarian composer and pianist. With Kodály studied Hungarian folk music. His most famous works include the Concerto for Orchestra and the opera *Bluebeard's Castle*.

Beach, Amy Marcy (1867-1944) American. Pianist and composer who was first president of the Association of Women Composers.

Beethoven, Ludwig van (1770-1827) German. Musical genius who spanned the end of the Classical and beginning of the Romantic periods. He wrote much chamber music including string quartets and piano music. He also composed nine symphonies, pushing the symphonic form to its limits.

Berg, Alban (1885-1935) Austrian. Pupil and friend of Schoenberg's. Wrote operas *Wozzeck* and *Lulu*.

Berio, Luciano (b. 1925) Italian composer. He has worked extensively with synthesizers, and often mixes musical instruments with pre-recorded tapes in his music.

Berlioz, Hector (1803-69) French. Romantic composer who wrote many large-scale works including the huge setting of the Requiem Mass, and the *Fantastic Symphony*.

Bernstein, Leonard (1918-90) American composer and conductor. Composer of *West Side Story*.

Bizet, Georges (1838-75) French composer most famous for his opera *Carmen*.

Boulanger, Nadia (1887-1979) French. Teacher and composer. Her sister Lili Boulanger (1893-1918) was the first woman to win the music prize called the Grand Prix de Rome, awarded by the Academy of Fine Arts in Paris, France.

Boulez, Pierre (b. 1925) Composer and conductor. Involved in setting up computer music studio in Paris called IRCAM.

Brahms, Johannes (1833-97) German. Romantic composer who wrote four symphonies as well as much chamber music.

Britten, Benjamin (1913-76) British composer and pianist. Famous for his operas such as *Peter Grimes* and *Albert Herring*.

Bruckner, Anton (1824-96) Austrian. Wrote nine symphonies as well as church music. Also an organist.

Byrd, William (c. 1542-1623) English. Worked at the Chapel Royal with Tallis. Wrote music for both Protestant and Catholic services

Cage, John (1912-92) American. Experimental composer who has influenced many 20th-century musicians.

Chopin, Frédéric (1810-49) Polish. Piano virtuoso and composer, famous for his piano music.

Johannes Brahms

Copland, Aaron (1900-90) American. Influenced by Stravinsky, but wrote music with an 'American' feel, such as *Appalachian Spring*.

Davies, Peter Maxwell (b. 1934) British composer. Helped to set up St Magnus Festival on islands of Orkney, Scotland and has written many pieces to be performed there.

Debussy, Claude (1862-1918) French composer who has influenced many composers and musicians in the 20th century.

Delius, Frederick (1862-1934) British composer. Studied in Leipzig and lived for much of his life in Grez-sur-Loing, France. Well-known for his orchestral evocations of nature in such works as *On hearing the first cuckoo in spring*.

Dufay, Guillaume (c. 1400-1474) Born in France. Composer who worked in the courts of France and Italy, travelling widely.

Dvořák, Antonín (1841-1904) Czech. Spent three years in America where he wrote the symphony 'From the New World'.

Elgar, Edward (1857-1934) British. Wrote many orchestral and choral works including *The Dream of Gerontius*, and the *Enigma Variations*.

Fauré, Gabriel (1845-1924) French. Wrote many songs and much piano music.

Gershwin, George (1898-1937) American. Composer who combined elements of jazz and classical music in works such as the opera *Porgy and Bess*, and the orchestral piece *Rhapsody in Blue*.

Glass, Philip (b. 1937) American. Studied amongst others with Nadia Boulanger and Ravi Shankar. Minimalist composer.

Grieg, Edvard (1843-1907) Norwegian composer. In much of his music influenced by folk styles and tunes of Norwegian music.

Handel, George Frideric (1685-1759) German. Wrote many oratorios, including *Messiah*, as well as operas. Worked in London for much of his life.

George Gershwin

Haydn, Joseph (1732-1809) Austrian composer. Kapellmeister at court of Prince Esterhazy for nearly 25 years.

Holst, Gustav (1874-1934) English composer. An influential teacher, his large-scale works include *A Hymn to Jesus* and, most famously, *The Planets*.

Janáček, Leoš (1854-1928) Czech composer. Studied Czech folk music and wrote many operas including *Jenufa, Katya Kabanova* and *The Cunning Little Vixen*.

Josquin, Desprez (c. 1440-1521) Flemish. Born in northern France, but worked in Italy for much of his life. He wrote 20 settings of the Catholic Mass.

Kodály, Zoltán (1882-1967) Hungarian composer who travelled around his country with Bartók, collecting and studying folk music.

Liszt, Franz (1811-86) Hungarian. Piano virtuoso, he rewrote many famous orchestral pieces for the piano.

Lully, Jean-Baptiste (1632-1687) Born in Florence, Italy, Lully rose to become the foremost French composer of his day. Worked at the court of Louis XIV of France.

Mahler, Gustav (1860-1911) Austrian. Wrote ten symphonies and many songs.

Leoš Janáček

Mendlessohn, Fanny (1805-47) German. Overshadowed by her famous brother, she had a few pieces published in her own lifetime.

Mendlessohn, Felix (1809-47) German. Composer and conductor, he revived many of Bach's works such as the *St Matthew Passion*.

Messiaen, Olivier (1908-92) French. Inspired by birdsong, ancient Indian music, the Roman Catholic church. He wrote many large-scale orchestral works and much organ music.

Milhaud, Darius (1892-1974) French composer who was very influenced by the rhythms and sounds of jazz music.

Monteverdi, Claudio (1567-1643) Italian. The first successful opera composer, his operas are still performed today.

Mozart, Wolfgang Amadeus (1756-91) Austrian. Genius of the Classical period, he wrote many symphonies and operas including *The Marriage of Figaro* and *Cosi fan Tutti*.

Musgrave, Thea (b. 1928) British. Studied with Nadia Boulanger. Has written several operas, including *Mary Queen of Scots*.

Mussorgsky, Modeste (1839-1881) Russian composer, friend of Rimsky-Korsakov. Most famous for his opera *Boris Godunov*.

da Palestrina, Giovanni Pierluigi (1525-94) Took his name from his birthplace in Italy. Wrote over 100 settings of the Catholic Mass.

Poulenc, Francis (1899-1963) French composer and pianist. Wrote *Mouvements perpetuels* for piano while he was serving in the army in World War I.

Prokofiev, Sergei (1891-1953) Russian. Pianist and composer. He wrote many symphonies, famous ballet music for *Romeo and Juliet*, and *Peter and the Wolf*.

Puccini, Giacomo (1858-1924) Italian. Known mainly for his operas including *La Bohème*, *Madame Butterfly* and *Tosca*.

Purcell, Henry (1658-95) English composer. Wrote church music, royal odes and theatre music including the opera *Dido and Aeneas*.

Sergei Prokofiev

Rachmaninov, Sergei (1873-1943) Russian. Virtuoso pianist as well as conductor and composer. His most famous works included his piano concertos and symphonies.

Ravel, Maurice (1875-1937) French. Like Debussy, he was influenced by Indonesian gamelan music heard at the Paris exhibition. Wrote ballets, songs and piano pieces.

Reich, Steve (b. 1936) American. Composer of minimalist music, he has studied with Berio and Milhaud and studied African drumming.

Rimsky-Korsakov, Nicolai (1844-1908) Nationalist Russian composer. Well-known for pieces such as the ballet *Scheherazade* and *The Flight of the Bumble Bee*.

Rossini, Gioacchino (1792-1868) Italian. Famous opera composer, including *The Barber of Seville*.

Schoenberg, Arnold (1874-1951) Austrian. Replaced system of using keys with a new system of 'tone-rows', a row of 12 notes on which a piece is based.

Schostakovich, Dmitri (1906-75) Russian. Wrote 15 symphonies as well as two operas and many film scores.

Schubert, Franz (1797-1828) Austrian. Famous for his songs, often known by their German name 'Leider', and chamber music.

Schumann, Clara (1819-96) German. Virtuoso pianist, also a composer.

Schumann, Robert (1810-56) German. Famous for his songs, piano music and symphonies.

Sibelius, Jean (1865-1957) Finnish. Wrote music about the landscapes and myths of his country, Finland.

Smetena, Bedřich (1824-1884) Czech composer. Influenced by the nationalist movement and wrote pieces entitled *Ma Vlast* (My Country) and *Vlatva* describing the river that flows through Prague.

Smyth, Ethel (1858-1944) British. Famous for her opera *The Wreckers*.

Stockhausen, Karlheinz (1928-1994) German. Composer and performer of electronic music, and works for orchestra, voice and others.

Strauss, Johann Jr (1825-99) Austrian composer, known as the 'Waltz-king'. One of a family of composers and conductors, he is remembered for his elegant waltzes such as *The Blue Danube*.

Strauss, Richard (1864-1949) German. One of the most Romantic of the 20th-century composers, famous for operas such as *Der Rosenkavalier*.

Stravinsky, Igor (1882-1971) Russian. Composer of the *Rite of Spring* as well as vocal pieces such as *Symphony of Psalms* and the ballet *Persephone*.

Igor Stravinsky

Tallis, Thomas (c. 1505-1585) English composer who was a member of the Chapel Royal with William Byrd. Wrote vocal music with both English and Latin words.

Takemitsu, Toru (1930-97) Japanese. Composed music with a mixture of Japanese and Western influences.

Tavener, John (b.1944) British. Composer influenced by the music and beliefs of the Russian Orthodox Church.

Tchaikovsky, Pyotr Ilyich (1840-93) Russian. Romantic composer of many famous orchestral works including *Romeo and Juliet* and '1812' overtures.

Tippett, Michael (1905-98) British. Composer of *A Child of Our Time* which makes use of spirituals. Also written four operas including *The Midsummer Marriage*.

Vaughan Williams, Ralph (1872-1958) British. Made use of English folksong in his music. Collected folksong from 1903 onwards.

Verdi, Giuseppe (1813-1901) Italian. Famous for his operas including *Aida* and *Rigoletto*. Also for his setting of the Requiem Mass.

Vivaldi, Antonio (1678-1741) Italian. Taught music at an orphanage in Venice and composed much music for his pupils. Most famous today for his concerto *The Four Seasons*.

Wagner, Richard (1813-1883) German. Famous for his large-scale operas on mythological themes, especially the *Ring* cycle.

Walton, William (1902-83) British. Wrote much orchestral and choral music including the oratorio *Belshazzar's Feast*.

Webern, Anton von (1883-1945) Austrian. Like Berg, a pupil of Schoenberg who experimented with tone-rows in his music.

Weill, Kurt (1900-50) German composer who became an American citizen in 1943. Weill's operas combine cabaret-style songs with dialogue and orchestral music. They include *The Rise and Fall of the City of Mahagonny*.

Weir, Judith (b. 1954) British. Operas include *The Vanishing Bridegroom*, *A Night at the Chinese Opera* and *Blond Eckbert*.

Franz Schubert (left) with musical friends

Index

A and B tunes 80
Aborigine music 31
AC/DC 69
accompaniment 16, 51, 55, 56, 72
acid house 69
acoustic instruments 44, 45, 47
Adams, John 68
aerophone 22
African music 11, 13, 23, 27, 34
  drumming 38, 39, 40, 68, 73
Alphorn 31
anvil 43
Arab music 18, 69
aria 57
Armstrong, Louis 65
art music 70
Australian music 31

Bach, Johann Sebastian 25, 55, 57
bagpipes 27
Balinese music 9
ballet 66
banjo 75
bar and barline 76
bard 72, 74
Baroque period 56-7
Bartók, Béla 73-4
bass clarinet 29
bass drum 40, 41, 43
bassoon 22, 27, 29
battle music 26, 30, 39, 70
Beach Boys 47
Beastie Boys 69
Beatles 14, 65, 77
Bee Gees 69
Beethoven, Ludwig van 19, 21, 33, 41, 55, 59-60
bells 35, 37-8, 42
Bennet, John 53
Berio, Luciano 49, 65
Berlioz, Hector 19, 41, 60, 61
Bernstein, Leonard 65
birdsong 67
Bizet, Georges 43
black music 67, 69, 71, 73
Black Sabbath 69

blues 67
Boehm, Theobald 25
Bon Jovi 69
bongos 41
Boulez, Pierre 49
bow 10, 11, 17
Bowie, David 69
Brahms, Johannes 19, 63
brass 22, 31-3
brass band 31, 33, 43
bridge 12, 15
Britten, Benjamin 46
broadcasting 68
Brookes, Garth 75
buccina 30
bugle 31
Bulgarian music 18
Burmese music 36
Byrd, William 50, 51, 54
Byrne, David 49

cabaca 34
Cage, John 49
calypso 37
car horn 43
Caribbean music 37, 73
carol 70
castanets 43
CD 65
cello 18, 19
ceremonial music 13, 57
chamber music 62-3
change ringing 37
Chieftains 75
Chinese music 15, 38, 72
Chopin, Frédéric 60, 61
chorale 54, 57
chordophone 10
chorus 56-7
church music see
  religious music
Clapton, Eric 45
clarinet 22, 26, 29
clarsach 72
Classical period 56, 58-9
clavichord 20
clef 19, 81-3
collecting folk music 73-4
compact disc 65
computer 44, 48, 49
concert 20, 58
conductor 64

consort 25
contrabassoon 29
Copland, Aaron 65
copying out 52
cor anglais 29
cornet 31
Country and Western 69, 75
court musicians 54, 56-7, 58
Covent Garden opera
  house 60
cradle song 70
crash cymbal 35, 41
Cristofori, Bartolomeo 20
crossbar 12
crotchet 78-9
cymbals 35, 43

dancing 27, 28, 54, 63, 72, 78
  ballet 66
  disco 69
  flamenco 16
  folk 35, 73-4
  Morris 35, 73
Debussy, Claude 65, 66
Denner, Johann 26
didgeridoo 31
disco 48, 65, 69
dotted note 79
double bass 10, 19, 82
double bassoon 22, 29
double clarinet 26
drone 18, 27, 51
drone strings 18
drum 28, 38-41, 68
drum kit 14, 35, 41, 75
drum machine 48, 69
drum pad 47
drumskin 38, 39, 40
Dufay, Guillaume 50, 51
Dvořák, Antonin 29, 33, 60, 64
Dylan, Bob 75

Egyptian music 10, 12, 30, 34
eisteddfod 74
electric guitar 14, 40, 44-5, 49, 69, 75

electronic music 9, 44, 46, 48, 65
Elgar, Edward 60, 64, 65
Eno, Brian 49
euphonium 31

Fairport Convention 75
Falla, Manuel de 16, 17
festivals 74
fiddle 17, 18, 72
fingerboard 14, 18
fingerhole 23, 26, 28, 31
flamenco dancing 16
flute 22-4, 28, 40, 52, 81, 82
folk music 16, 63, 64, 67, 70-5
folk-rock 69, 75
French horn 22, 31, 32, 33
fret 11
Fripp, Robert 45
funk 48

Gabriel, Peter 9, 49
gagaku 28
gamelan 36-7, 66, 68
Gershwin, George 29, 33, 65
glam rock 65, 69
Glass, Philip 65, 68
glockenspiel 42, 43, 68
gong 35, 36, 41, 43
gong chime 36
gospel music 71
gourd 14
grand piano 21, 61
Grand-master Flash 69
Greek music 12, 18, 30, 34
Gregorian chant 50
Grieg, Edvard 29, 60, 64
guitar 10, 11, 16, 17, 40, 75
gypsy music 20

Handel, George Frideric 33, 56
harp 10, 12-13, 51, 72
harpsichord 20, 49
Hawaiian guitar 75
Haydn, Joseph 55, 57, 58,

62, 64
Haza, Ofra 69
heavy metal 65, 69
Hendrix, Jimi 45
hi-hat cymbal 35, 41
hichikiri 28
Hiller, Lejaren 49
Holst, Gustav 74
house music 65
Hungarian music 20, 73-4
hunting horn 32, 33

idiophone 34
Indian music 14, 24, 27, 41, 83
Indonesian music 36, 66, 68
Iron Maiden 69

Janáček, Leoš 64, 74
Japanese music 15, 25, 28, 38, 39-40, 71
Jarre, Jean-Michel 49
jazz 16, 19, 33, 35, 41
  saxophone 27, 29, 67
jingles 34, 35, 40
Joplin, Scott 65, 67, 77
Josquin Desprez 50, 51
juju 40, 69

kalengo 40
keyboard 20-1, 61, 83
keys (for fingers) 28, 29, 31
kit (pocket fiddle) 18
ko-tsuzumi 40
Kodály, Zoltán 73-4
koto 15, 28

Lambert, Constant 21
ländler 63
ledger line 81
lira da braccio 18
Liszt, Franz 43, 60, 61
lituus 30
Lloyd Webber, Andrew 19, 77
Lully, Jean-Baptiste 55
lute 16, 28, 52
lyre 12, 13, 51

McTell, Ralph 75
madrigal 50, 52-3
Mahler, Gustav 65
major scale 83
making instruments 17,

22, 23
marching 30
marimba 46, 68
Marley, Bob 73
mass (church) 50, 51, 54
materials for making
  instruments 12, 20, 22
  animal hair and skin 11, 17, 38, 39, 40
  bone and horn 23, 32, 34
  cane 26-7
  clay 23
  gourd 11, 14
  metal 22, 25, 29, 30, 31, 32
  oil drum 12
  plants 11, 26-7, 34
  shell 11, 32, 34
  wood 10, 22, 42
May, Brian 44, 45
maypole dance 73
melody 51, 80
membranophone 34
Mendelssohn, Fanny 62
Mendelssohn, Felix 60-2
Messiaen, Olivier 47, 65, 67
metallophone 37
metronome 77
MIDI 49
Milhaud, Darius 46
minim 78-9
minimalist music 68
minor scale 83
minstrels 51
Monteverdi, Claudio 55
mood music 60-1
Morris dancing 35, 73
motown 65, 69
mouth organ 28, 75
mouthpiece 22, 23, 26, 27, 29, 31
movements of symphony 58
Mozart, Wolfgang
  Amadeus 19, 55, 62
  family 59
  symphonies 29, 58, 64
Musica Transalpina 50, 52
musique concréte 48-9

nationalism 64
N'Dour, Youssou 69
Noh theatre 39-40
nose-flute 24

oboe 22, 27, 28, 29
octet 62
ondes martenot 46, 47, 67
opera 55, 58, 60, 64, 72
oratorio 56-7
orchestra 8, 33, 36-7, 64
organ 30, 57
Orpheus and Eurydice 12, 55
Osibisa 69
ostinato 68
overture 61

Pakistani music 27
Palestrina, Giovanni da 50, 51, 54
panpipes 23, 24
part song 80
part writing 51, 52
Parton, Dolly 75
Passion oratorios 57
patronage 57, 58
peal of bells 37
percussion 28, 34-43, 79
p'i p'a 15
piano 20, 21, 61, 83
piccolo 22, 25
pitch 10-11, 22, 34, 36, 37, 81-2
pizzicato 17
plainsong 50, 51, 53-4
planting songs 71
plectrum 10, 14, 15, 20
plucking 12, 14, 15, 16, 17, 19
Polynesian music 24
polyphony 50, 51, 52
pon 40
pop 16, 29, 35, 44-5, 48-9, 68-9
printing 50, 52
programme music 60-1, 64
Prokofiev, Sergei 33, 65
Puccini, Giacomo 65
pulse 76-8
pungi 26
punk 65, 69
Purcell, Henry 28

qin 15
quartet 62
quaver 78-9

Queen (group) 44
quintet 62

ragtime 67
rap 65, 69
rattle 34
rave 65, 69
rebab 18
rebec 18
recorder 25
reed 24, 26, 27, 29, 31
reel (dance) 72
Reformation 53
reggae 69, 73
Reich, Steve 65, 68
religious music 32, 73
  Africa 34, 50
  China 38, 50
  India 27, 50
  Japan 38-9, 50
  Western 50-1, 53-4, 56-7, 58
Renaissance 53
resonator 11-12, 15, 16, 38, 42
  electric instruments 44, 45, 46
rest 79
rhythm 66, 78-9
ride cymbal 41
Rimsky-Korsakov, Nikolai 64
rock 16, 40, 41, 44-5, 49, 68
Rodrigo, Joaquin 16
Roman music 11, 30, 34
Romantic style 60-4, 65
Ronstadt, Linda 75
Ross, Diana 69

sackbut 32
Saint-Saëns, Camille 43
sampling 47-8, 49
saxophone 26, 27, 29, 60, 67
scale 83
Schubert, Franz 19, 60, 62-3
Schumann, Clara 60, 62
Schumann, Robert 63
Scottish music 27, 72
Seeger, Pete 75
Segovia, Andre[']s 16
semibreve 78-9
semiquaver 78-9
semitone 82-3
sequencer 47, 48, 49

Sex Pistols 69
shahnai 27
Shankar, Ravi 14
shanty 70
sharp 83
Sharp, Cecil 74
shawm 27-28
sho 28
Sibelius, Jean 60, 64
side drum 40-1
side-blown flute 24, 25
signalling music 31, 32, 39
Simon and Garfunkel 75
singing 16, 22
  chorus 56-7, 80
  Country and Western 75
  electronic music 47, 48
  folk 70-5
  madrigal 52-3
  minstrels 51
sistrum 34
sitar 14
slide 32
slit drum 38-9
Smetana, Bedrich 64
snake-charmers 26
snare drum 41, 43
sopranino recorder 25
sorrow song 71
sound effects 49
sound post 11
sound tracks 49
soundbox 14, 20
sousaphone 31

South American music 23, 34
Spandau Ballet 69
Spanish music 16, 73
spiritual 71
stave 80-2
steel drums 37
Steeleye Span 75
Stockhausen, Karlheinz 48, 65
stopping 11, 18
Stradivari, Antonio 18, 55
Strauss, Johann 8, 63
Strauss, Richard 41, 64, 65
Stravinsky, Igor 29, 65, 66
Sumer is icumen in 50, 52
Sumerian music 12, 13, 27
Summers, Andy 45
Supremes 69
suspended cymbal 35
Sweet (glam rock) 69
Switzerland 31
sympathetic strings 14, 15
symphony 58
syncopation 77, 86
synthesizer 44, 47, 49

tabla 41
Tabor, June 75
talking drums 40

Tallis, Thomas 54
tambourine 40, 43
tango 78
tape recording 48, 49, 68
Tchaikovsky, Pyotr 13, 42
telharmonium 44, 46
temple bells 38
Thai music 36, 42
theme 67
theremin 44, 46, 47
Thompson, Richard 75
thunder sheet 43
timpani 40, 41
tom-tom drums 41
tone 82
Townsend, Pete 45
triangle 43
trombone 22, 31, 32, 33
troubadours 50, 51
trumpet 22, 30, 31, 33
tuba 22, 30, 31, 33
tubular bells 42, 43
tune (melody) 80
tuned percussion 34, 40, 41
tuning 10-11, 12, 13, 40
tuning peg 11, 12, 13, 16, 18

untuned percussion 34
unusual instruments 43
upright piano 61

Vai, Steve 45
valve 30, 31, 32, 33

Vaughan Williams, Ralph 29, 74
vibraphone 46
vibration 10-12, 22, 23, 26, 27
vina 14
viola 18, 19
violin 10, 11, 17, 18, 19, 75
voice see singing
volume 9

Wagner, Richard 33
waltz 63
Weavers 75
Weelkes, Thomas 53
Welsh music 74
whistle 23
Wolf, Hugo 63
women musicians 62
Wonder, Stevie 69
woodwind 22, 31
word-painting 53
working songs 70-1
world music 69
written music 8, 50, 51, 70, 74
  jazz 67
  stave 80-2

xylophone 37, 42, 43, 68

Zappa, Frank 45
zither 15

Internet links

You can find out more about different styles of music by looking at the following websites:

www.classical.net/music/
http://music.top10sites.net/
www.jdscomm.com/jazz1.html
www.eyeneer.com/World/
www.obsolete.com/120-years/
http://realworld.on.net/womad/
www.medieval.org/
www.musicink.co.uk/